English for Fun

Fremdsprachentexte | Englisch

English for Fun

Von Andrew Williams und Ruth Kletzander
Mit Illustrationen von Rosalie Kletzander

Reclam

RECLAMS UNIVERSAL-BIBLIOTHEK Nr. 19887

Gesamtherstellung: Reclam, Ditzingen. Printed in Germany 2016

ISBN 978-3-15-019887-2
www.reclam.de

Inhalt

Foreword

English Can Be Fun!

English has become a global language. All over the world people use English for a variety of activities including negotiating in business settings, studying, travelling, and surfing on the Internet. However, because people are often so busy using the language they have little time to stop and have fun with it. This is a pity. It is actually great fun to play with language.

English for Fun gives people a chance to play with English. It aims to help people become familiar with colourful idioms, funny euphemisms as well as famous quotes which shed light on the cultures of native English speakers. In fact, even what we consider funny is influenced by where we grew up. For example, there is a considerable difference between what Britons, Australians, and Americans find funny. This is sometimes just a matter of vocabulary, but it is often related to cultural taboos. *English for Fun* presents a variety of funny entries from different English-speaking countries, but it is not meant to be comprehensive. It is a sampler.

English is also funny when it goes wrong … And there is a lot that can go wrong with language. This book 'takes the mickey' out of English speakers' own writing as they often misspell, use commas incorrectly and write ambiguous sentences, which can completely change the meaning from what they intended.

But even when it is perfectly correct, there are some words

11 f. **to shed light on s.th.** (fig.): Aufschluss über etwas geben, etwas erhellen (*shed – shed – shed*). | 17 **entry:** Eintrag. | 19 **comprehensive:** vollständig, umfassend. | 21 f. **to take the mickey out of s.o.** (BE, coll.): jdn. auf den Arm / die Schippe nehmen. | 23 **ambiguous:** mehrdeutig.

that simply sound funny from the very beginning such as 'boondoggle', 'kerfuffle', and 'squeegee'. And there are idioms that evoke a funny image, including 'to open a can of worms' or 'to stick your foot in your mouth'. But funny can refer to more than something that simply makes us laugh.

Saying, 'that sounds funny, doesn't it?' reflects a sudden awareness that something sounds strange. (Germans would say *komisch.*) *English for Fun* takes this aspect of funny into account. Actually, the closer we look at language, the funnier it becomes. Everybody has experienced this: choose any word you like and repeat it twenty times. Eventually the word starts to sound, well, funny.

Classroom Use

English for Fun can be used to lighten up lessons, as well as for casual reading. People everywhere enjoy the silliness of language – all the more reason to include it in the classroom. Tongue twisters can help learners to make their pronunciation and rhythm sound more natural. Riddles are an excellent way of learning idioms, as riddles often play with the literal and figurative meanings of idioms, and idioms can be a window into the culture of native speakers!

Last but not least, *English for Fun* provides opportunities for expanding students' vocabulary. In particular, this book contains collections of words and idioms that sound funny and are used frequently. Native speakers know these expressions 'like

3 **to evoke:** hervorrufen, evozieren. | 8 f. **to take s.th. into account:** etwas berücksichtigen, etwas beachten. | 14 **to lighten up:** hier: auflockern. | 15 **casual** ['kæʒjʊəl] **reading:** Freizeitlektüre. | 17 **tongue twister:** Zungenbrecher. | 18 **riddle:** Rätsel.

the back of their hands'. If you want to find out how often some of these funny words and expressions are used in everyday speech, then just spend some time listening to a group of native speakers. Sooner or later they will say 'gobbledygook', 'gazillion' or 'gizmo', to name just a few examples. This is equally true of written language. Words like 'bloviate', 'boondoggle' and 'brouhaha' are commonly used in newspapers and news magazines.

English for Fun, then, is not just intended to make readers laugh; it is a resource for teachers who want to add some fun to their lessons.

That Sounds Funny …

Strange-sounding words, rhyming just for the fun of it, noises animals make, tongue twisters and more …

caboodle cahoots canoodle codswallop collywobbles …

3 **tongue twister:** Zungenbrecher.

Funny-Sounding Words

English has lots of words that simply sound, well, funny. Most native speakers use these words and don't think they sound unusual at all until you draw their attention to them. Once you read the list, you'll start noticing them – and why not try using some of them yourself?

balderdash nonsense. (See also **codswallop**.) *His excuse for coming late was complete balderdash.*

bamboozle deceive or confuse. *He bamboozled his enemies with an unexpected action.*

bedraggled dishevelled, untidy, messy. *After falling in the swimming pool, the cat looked bedraggled.*

bloviate (AE) to talk about something at length in an arrogant manner without saying much. *Politicians love bloviating about their reforms.*

boondocks (AE) also **boonies** backwoods, a remote rural area. (See also **woop-woop** [AusE], p. 27.) *He lives way out of town – somewhere in the boondocks.*

boondoggle (AE) a project that is a waste of time and money. *Unfortunately, the new airport will be a boondoggle.*

brouhaha an uproar in reaction to an event, speech, decision, etc. *It's hard to believe there has been so much brouhaha about same-sex marriage.*

caboodle 'the whole kit and caboodle' is a complete collection of things. *I didn't just lose my phone. I lost the headphones, the adapter, the charger, the case – the whole kit and caboodle.*

4 **to draw s.o.'s attention to s.th.:** jdn. auf etwas aufmerksam machen. | 11 **dishevelled** [dɪˈʃevəld]: unordentlich, zerzaust. | 17 f. **way out of town:** sehr weit draußen vor der Stadt. | 21 **uproar:** Aufruhr, Tumult. | 26 **charger:** Ladegerät.

cahoots to be 'in cahoots with' is to be partners in a shady, dubious, or illegal activity. *The Tour de France cyclists were in cahoots with the race organizers.*

canoodle (BE, AusE) to kiss and hug. *There was a bit of canoodling at the high school party.*

codswallop nonsense. (See also **balderdash**.) *What a load of codswallop!*

collywobbles (BE, AusE) a feeling in your stomach due to nervousness or fear. *I had the collywobbles before the job interview.*

diddlysquat not anything at all. Always used in a negative sentence: *I don't know diddlysquat about economics.* Or: *I don't know diddly about economics.* Or even: *I don't know squat about it.*

discombobulated confused and upset. *When he woke up from the coma he was discombobulated.*

dollop a shapeless lump of something, usually cream. Also as a verb: *He dolloped out the cream.*

doozy (AE) something that is extraordinary or very serious for its kind. *That tornado was a doozy* (a very strong one). *That flu was a doozy* (a very bad one). *That test was a doozy* (a very difficult one).

flabbergasted so surprised or shocked that you don't know what to say. *I was flabbergasted when she told me her twelve-year-old was pregnant.* (See also **gobsmacked**.)

flapdoodle (AE) meaningless talk. *That cell phone conversation I heard on the train was nothing but flapdoodle.*

flummoxed puzzled, perplexed. *He was flummoxed by her behaviour and didn't know how to respond.*

1 **shady** (coll.): zwielichtig, fragwürdig. | 4 **to hug:** sich umarmen. | 17 **lump:** Klumpen. | 28 **puzzled:** verdutzt, verblüfft.

gazebo a garden house with lots of windows. *They enjoyed chatting over a lovely cup of tea in the gazebo.*

gazillion an extremely large, but unspecified, number, quantity, or amount. *There were a gazillion people at the Oktoberfest on Saturday.*

gizmo a small gadget or device. *He had a great little gizmo for opening locked car doors.*

gobbledygook language that is so complicated and full of jargon that it becomes impossible to understand. (Similar to **codswallop**.) *Most post-structuralist theory is gobbledygook, if you ask me.*

gobsmacked (BE, AusE) so surprised that you don't know what to say. (See also **flabbergasted**.) *She was gobsmacked when the doctor gave her the results of the test.*

hornswoggle (See **bamboozle**.) *The Internet scammer hornswoggled lots of people out of their money before he got caught.*

hubbub the noise a crowd makes. *There was so much hubbub at the party I couldn't hear myself think.*

hullaballoo a loud reaction to an event. (See also **brouhaha**.) *There was a hullaballoo about the referee's decision.*

jiggery-pokery (BE) manipulation, either deceitful: *The president won the election by jiggery-pokery*; or any other kind of manipulation: *Unlocking your smart phone involves a bit of jiggery-pokery.*

kerfuffle (BE) a fuss or commotion. *There was a big kerfuffle about the Royal Family not paying taxes.*

lackadaisical unenthusiastic, idle. *You'll never get anywhere in life with your lackaduisical attitude.*

6 **gadget:** Gerät, Apparat. | 15 **scammer** (coll.): Betrüger(in). | 22 **deceitful:** betrügerisch. | 26 **fuss:** Getue. | **commotion:** Wirbel, Aufregung. | 28 **idle:** faul, träge.

lickety-split immediately, without delay. *Don't worry. I'll take care of that lickety-split.*

mollycoddle (BE) to spoil or pamper someone. *Today's children are mollycoddled.*

nincompoop an idiot, a fool. *The boss is a complete nincompoop when it comes to communication.*

pernickety (BE), **persnickety** (AE) very inflexible, fussy. *He is very pernickety about grammar rules.* As a noun: *His pernicketiness knows no limits.*

rambunctious uncontrollably excited. *That child gets rambunctious when he eats too much chocolate.*

ramshackle in very bad physical condition. *They lived in a ramshackle house that was* ***on its last legs****.* (See p. 69.)

razzmatazz showiness. (See also **razzle-dazzle**, p. 26.) *That politician is known for his razzmatazz in speeches, but not for keeping his promises.*

shebang 'the whole shebang' is everything, all of it. (See **caboodle**.) *At the flea market, I found lots of LPs at one stand and decided to buy the whole shebang.*

shenanigans misbehaviour. *The boys were up to their usual shenanigans when the teacher left the classroom.*

skedaddle to run away, flee, leave quickly. *When her ex-boyfriend showed up at the party, she skedaddled out the back door.*

skew-whiff (BE) crooked, not straight. *She adjusted his tie because it was skew-whiff.*

skulduggery trickery, dishonest behaviour. *If you look closely, there is a lot of skulduggery in the stock market.*

3 **to pamper:** verwöhnen, verhätscheln. | 7 **fussy:** pingelig, kleinlich. | 14 **showiness:** Effekthascherei, Geprahle. | 25 **crooked** ['krʊkɪd]: krumm. | **to adjust:** in Ordnung bringen; hier: (Krawatte) zurechtrücken.

smithereens small fragments caused by an explosion. *The land mine blew the truck to smithereens.*

squeegee an object with a handle and a rubber edge that you use to clean windows.

wazoo (AE) butt, ass. As in: *a pain in the wazoo*. With *up* or *out* it can mean 'in excess'. *Germans are insured out the wazoo.* (In other words, Germans have far too much insurance.) *When the president came to town there was security up the wazoo.* (In other words, there were police everywhere.)

whirligig something that spins. It can also refer to any **gizmo** or strange piece of rotating technical equipment. *The scientist's laboratory was full of whirligigs.*

Elephant's at the Rubbity: Rhyming Slang

What does it mean when someone says everything is 'apples'? What if someone calls you a 'berk'? And what should you do if an Australian tells you it's high time you changed your 'Reginalds'?

The key to these puzzling expressions is something called 'rhyming slang', a kind of slang that originated in East London to confuse listeners who were outsiders. It is understood and used not only in Britain, but also in Australia, South Africa and New Zealand. (Americans, however, are generally not familiar with rhyming slang.)[1]

1 One reason for the popularity or at least general acceptance of rhyming slang in Australia may be the fact it was used among convicts and spread by them as they were shipped out to the Australian penal colonies.

5 **butt / ass** (AE, coll.): Arsch. | 18 **puzzling:** rätselhaft. | 19 **to originate** [əˈrɪdʒɪneɪt]: entstehen.

How does it work? You simply replace a word (it can be any word you like, but it is usually an everyday word) with a phrase of two or three words that rhymes with it. 'Head', for example, rhymes with 'loaf of *bread*'. So if you want to tell someone to use their head (in other words: to think), you might say 'use your loaf of bread'. The next step is to leave out the rhyming word, so that the end result is:

'Use your loaf!'

People who are not familiar with rhyming slang will find this incomprehensible. A second example: we could replace 'look' with 'butcher's *hook*'. So if you want to take a look at the newspaper you could say, 'I'm going to take a butcher's at the newspaper.'

A relatively recent example involves **Reginald** (or 'Reg') Grundy, a very successful television producer, whose name became a household word in Australia in the 1980s.

'You need to change your Reginalds.'

As 'Grundys' rhymes with 'undies' (underpants), some Australians started saying 'Reg Grundys' instead of 'undies'. As in the example above ('loaf'), the rhyming word is left out, so finally you end up with 'reggies' or 'Reginalds'.

As far as **'berk'** goes, it comes from the **'Berkley hunt'**, a group of hunting hounds (with a very long history) from Berkshire in England. 'Hunt' rhymes with an English four-letter ob-

10 **incomprehensible:** unverständlich, unbegreiflich. | 16 **household word:** Alltagsausdruck, (fester) Begriff. | 22 **as far as (that) goes:** was (das) betrifft. | 24 f. **four letter (…) -unt:** *cunt* (vulg.): Fotze, Möse; (fig., pej.) Arsch.

scenity that begins with 'c-' and ends in '-unt'. So if somebody calls you a 'berk', it is an insult – although in most cases it simply means 'idiot'. See if you can figure out these examples of rhyming slang:

Run up the **apples** and get on the **dog** to your **trouble**.

apples [and pears]	stairs
dog [and bone]	telephone
trouble [and strife]	wife

I'm wearing a **bag of fruit** to the interview tomorrow.

bag of fruit	suit

'Oh, so I have to look after the **saucepan lids** and do the housework while you enjoy yourself at the **rubbity** and get **elephant's** – that's very **apples and rice**.'

saucepan [lids]	kids
rubbity [dub]	pub
elephant's [trunk]	drunk
apples [and rice]	nice

Hey **china**, how ya goin'? (AusE)

china [plate]	mate

I spent the whole weekend sitting around on my **Khyber**.

Khyber [Pass]	arse

8 **strife:** Zwietracht, Streit. | 16 **trunk:** Rüssel. | 18 **china:** Porzellan. | **how ya goin'?** (sl.): wie geht's? (*ya* [coll.]: you). | 21 **Khyber Pass:** Chaiber-Pass (Bergpass zwischen Pakistan und Afghanistan). | **arse** (BE, sl.): Arsch.

Tourists who visit Australia are often afraid of **Joe Blakes** and **Noah's Arks.**

Joe Blake	snake
Noah's Ark	shark

"Hasta luego cocodrilo"

You may have noticed that the title of this section is in Spanish. "Hasta luego cocodrilo" is the Spanish version of a song by Bill Haley & His Comets from the year 1955. The original title was "See you later, alligator", followed by "After 'while, crocodile". This saying has become very popular and is still used today in America. Elsewhere, it is usually like this:

A: See you later, alligator!
B: In a while, crocodile!

Children love this sort of rhyming game. Here are 'some more, department store':

No way, José!

Far out, Brussels sprout!

What's the deal, banana peel?

What's cookin', good lookin'?

4 **shark:** Hai. | 10 **saying:** Redensart. | 16 **no way:** niemals!, vergiss es! | 17 **far out:** super, toll. | **Brussels sprout:** Rosenkohl. | 18 **what's the deal?** (coll.): worum geht's? | 19 **what's cookin'?** (coll.): was ist los?

What's up, buttercup?

What's the plan, Stan?

Okey-dokey, artichokey!

Don't panic, Titanic!

Tongue Twisters

In German you break your tongue; in English, you twist it. For a little tongue tango try these:

Unique New York.

A noisy noise annoys an oyster.

The sixth sheik's sixth sheep is sick.

Nine nimble noblemen nibbling nuts.

Sally sells sea shells by the sea shore.

Sam's shop stocks short spotted socks.

Six slippery snails slid slowly seaward.

Fred fed Ted bread and Ted fed Fred bread.

1 **buttercup:** Butterblume. | 3 **okey-dokey:** okay. | 8 **unique** [juːˈniːk]: einzigartig, einmalig. | 9 **oyster:** Auster. | 10 **sheik(h)** [ʃeɪk]: Scheich. | 11 **nimble:** flink, behende, geschickt. | **nobleman:** Adliger. | **to nibble:** knabbern. | 12 **shell:** Muschel. | 14 **to slide:** rutschen, gleiten (*slide – slid – slid*).

How much wood would a woodchuck chuck
if a woodchuck could chuck wood?

A skunk sat on a stump and thunk the stump stunk, but the stump thunk the skunk stunk too.[2]

The big black bug bit the big black bear
but the big black bear bit the big black bug back.

To begin to toboggan first buy a toboggan. But do not buy too big a toboggan. Too big a toboggan is too big a toboggan to buy to begin to toboggan.

Theodore Oswaldtwistle, the thistle sifter, sifting a sack of thistles, thrust three thorns through the thick of his thumb.

Betty Botter had some butter, 'But,' she said, 'this butter's bitter! If I bake this bitter butter, it would make my batter bitter. But a bit of better butter – that would make my batter better.' So she bought a bit of butter, better than her bitter butter, and she baked it in her batter, and the batter was not bitter. So 'twas better Betty Botter bought a bit of better butter.

The following tongue twisters have an additional twist. Try saying them slowly at first. Then increase the tempo until you say something you didn't actually want to say …

2 'Thunk' is a playful past participle of 'think'. After all, if you say 'drink – drank – drunk', why not 'think – thank – thunk'?

1 **woodchuck:** Waldmurmeltier. | **to chuck:** schmeißen, werfen. | 5 **bug:** Insekt. | 7 **to toboggan** [tə'bɒgən]: Schlitten fahren, rodeln. | 10 **thistle sifter:** »Distelsieber(in)« (*thistle:* Distel; *to sift:* sieben). | 11 **to thrust:** stechen; stoßen (*thrust – thrust – thrust*). | 13 **batter:** (Ausback-, Pfannkuchen-)Teig.

One smart man, he felt smart.

I'm not a fig plucker or a fig plucker's son. But I'll pluck figs till the fig plucker comes.

I slit a sheet, a sheet I slit and on that slitted sheet I sit.

I am a pheasant plucker, a pheasant plucker's son, and I'll be plucking pheasants till all the pheasant plucking's done.

Two Witches

There was a witch
The witch had an itch
The itch was so itchy it
Gave her a twitch.

Another witch
Admired the twitch
So she started twitching
Though she had no itch.

Now both of them twitch
So it's hard to tell which
Witch has the itch and
Which witch has the twitch.[3]

Alexander Resnikoff

3 Davies, John (ed.), *Everyman's Book of Nonsense*, London: Dent, 1981, p. 187.

2 **fig plucker:** Feigenpflücker(in). | 4 **to slit:** (auf)schlitzen (*slit – slit – slit*). | 5 **pheasant** ['fezənt] **plucker:** Fasanenrupfer(in). | 9 **itch:** Juckreiz. | 11 **twitch:** Zucken; Zuckung.

Wishy-Washy, Arty-Farty

Things like 'wishy-washy' and 'willy-nilly' are called reduplications. A reduplication is simply a repetition of a syllable – with or without a slight change. English has literally hundreds of them. Some of them can be used as verbs ('dilly-dally'), but most of them function as adjectives or nouns. Believe it or not: people use these all the time!

airy-fairy not concerned with reality; vague, impractical. *He has an airy-fairy plan to save the rainforests.*

arty-farty (BE) / **artsy fartsy** (AE) pretentious, acting as if interested in the arts. *I'm sick of your arty-farty pseudo-intellectual friends.*

argy-bargy (BE) a lively, but not serious, argument. Also used as an adjective: *You don't need to get all argy-bargy about it!*

bric-a-brac old, worthless stuff used as decoration. *The old woman decorated the entire house with bric-a-brac.*

chit-chat, chitter chatter light conversation, gossip, 'hot air'. *I don't have time for her endless chit-chat.*

claptrap (BE) insincere or pretentious talk, nonsense *Everything he says is claptrap.*

dilly-dally to waste time, faff around. *No dilly-dallying!*

easy-peasy (BE) very simple. *That test was easy-peasy.*

flip-flop (AE) to constantly change your opinion. *That politician is known for his flip-flopping on issues.*

fuddy-duddy an old-fashioned person. *He's such an old fuddy-duddy, he never wants to try anything new.*

10 **pretentious:** überheblich, prätentiös. | 20 **insincere:** unaufrichtig. | 22 **to faff around:** Zeit vertrödeln.

goody-goody someone who never breaks the rules. *At school she's a goody-goody, but at home ... watch out!*

hanky-panky sexual misbehaviour: kissing, cuddling and groping. *No hanky-panky!*

heebie-jeebies to feel nervously uncomfortable or slightly scared. *The way he looked at me gave me the heebie-jeebies.* (See also **the creeps**, p. 117.)

helter-skelter in a confused way. In Britain, it also refers to a spiral slide at an amusement park. *The people ran helter-skelter when they heard the gunshots at the demonstration.*

higgledy-piggledy chaotic, disorganized. *It's no wonder he can never find anything: he throws everything on his desk higgledy-piggledy.*

hob-nob to rub elbows with, to **schmooze** (see p. 83) with, to chat with influential people hoping that they will do you favours. *I went to opening night to do some hob-nobbing.*

hocus-pocus magic formula; or deceit or trickery. *The government balanced the budget using a bit of hocus-pocus.*

hoity-toity arrogant, snobbish. *That rich woman had a hoity-toity look on her face.*

hodgepodge a disorganized set of things. *There used to be a hodgepodge of currencies in Europe.*

hurly-burly refers to loud activity, commotion, or noisy confusion. *Some people love the hurly-burly of the Oktoberfest.* (Compare with **helter-skelter**.)

2 **to watch out:** aufpassen, sich vorsehen. | 4 **groping** (coll.): Fummeln. | 14 **to rub elbows with s.o.:** mit jdm. – besonders mit einflussreichen Menschen – Umgang/Kontakt haben. | 16 **opening night:** Eröffnungsvorstellung, Premiere. | 18 **deceit:** Täuschung; Betrug. | 19 **to balance the budget:** den Haushalt ausgleichen. | 24 **commotion:** Unruhe, Wirbel.

incy-wincy, eensie-weensie, itsy-bitsy, itty-bitty, teenie-weenie, teensie-weensie tiny. *It was an eensie-weensie tick that gave him the disease.*

knick-knack little kitschy things used for decoration. Like **bric-a-brac** but smaller. *She had lots of knick-knacks on the shelf.*

mish-mash a bunch of things thrown together. (See also **hodgepodge**.)

mumbo-jumbo talk that doesn't make much sense; language with a lot of jargon. *Everything the doctor said was mumbo-jumbo to me.*

namby-pamby (BE) weak or indecisive, too gentle. *The namby-pamby treatment of criminals was* ***pooh-poohed*** *by the press.*

nitty-gritty the practical details of something, for example negotiations: *I think we agree on the main points, now let's get down to the nitty-gritty.*

no-no something forbidden. *Texting while driving is a big no-no.*

pitter-patter soft, repetitive noise. For example: rain on the roof, or small children running. If someone asks, '*When will we be hearing the pitter-patter of little feet?*' it means they want to know when you are going to have children.

pooh-pooh to express your disrespect for something. *He is always pooh-poohing astrology.*

razzle-dazzle glamorous excitement, sparkly, glittery appearance. *She loved the razzle-dazzle of Las Vegas.*

rumpy-pumpy sexual intercourse. *Their squeaky bed let the whole house know they were up to some rumpy-pumpy.*

3 **tick** (zool.): Zecke. | 12 **indecisive:** unentschlossen. | 26 **sparkly:** funkelnd.

ship-shape in good order, tidy and organized. *They made sure the house was ship-shape before they went on holiday.*

silly-billy someone acting foolishly. *Don't be such a silly-billy.*

sing-song a way of talking that sounds like a melody. *Norwegian has a sing-song intonation.*

topsy-turvy upside down, confused. *In Alice in Wonderland everything is topsy-turvy.*

willy-nilly randomly when it should be well-ordered. *He threw his clean clothes willy-nilly in the drawer.*

wishy-washy vague and imprecise. *Palm readers make wishy-washy predictions about the future.*

woop-woop (AusE) is a long way away. *He lives out woop-woop.* (See also **boondocks**, p. 13.)

zig-zag a line that is like a lightning bolt. *Today all sewing machines have a zig-zag stitch.*

New reduplications are being created all the time. They reflect our changing lifestyle. Here are some recent, trendy coinages. (Okay, if there are any linguists reading this: these are not really reduplications, just words that rhyme.)

bi-guy a bisexual male.

blame game an endless discussion about who is at fault.

bricks 'n' clicks a business model involving a mixture of offline (bricks) and online (clicks) presence.

cell yell talking loudly on a cell phone in a public place.

chalk 'n' talk a traditional method of teaching: write something on the blackboard and then talk about it. Also known

9 **randomly:** wahllos, willkürlich. | 15 **lightning bolt:** Blitzschlag. | 18 **coinage** (fig.): Prägung, Neuschöpfung. | 22 **to be at fault:** schuld sein.

as 'sage on the stage' (teacher-centred) as opposed to 'guide on the side' (student-centred teaching).

chick-flick a film aimed at female audiences. For example: *Sex and the City*.

culture vulture someone keen on high culture. A culture vulture never misses a premiere or opening night.

fat cat a rich and powerful businessman, typically fat and smoking a cigar.

pooper-scooper a tool for picking up pet poop.

rich bitch negative term for an unpleasant, rich woman.

snail mail ordinary mail as opposed to e-mail (used for the first time by some computer nerds back in 1982).

boy toy / toy boy a young man who is dating a much older woman.

Fancy Schmancy

> 'I have to tell you, madam, that your son is suffering from an Oedipus complex.'
> 'Oedipus, Schmoedipus! What does it matter, so long as he loves his mother?'
> (Jewish joke)

A very special case of reduplication has been borrowed from Yiddish into English. It is like a word game that can be done with practically any word. It works like this: the word is duplicated, but the first consonant or consonants are dropped and replaced with 'schm-'. Mostly this reduplication is done with words accented on the first syllable. This gives you 'present schmesent', 'happy schmappy', 'table schmable', and so on.

1 **sage:** Weise(r). | 9 **poop** (coll.): Kacke.

These reduplications are not just a way of playing with the language, they playfully poke fun at what someone has said. They are often used to deflate pretension:

'It's a very fancy restaurant.'
'**Fancy schmancy** – just because **it costs an arm and a leg** (see p. 70) to eat there doesn't mean it's got good food.'

They can also be used to show scepticism:

'She thinks she has mononucleosis.'
'**Mononucleosis schmononucleosis**. She's just a hypochondriac.'

Or to indicate something is ridiculous:

'You can't expect him to tie his own shoes. He's only in kindergarten.'
'**Kindergarten schmindergarten**. He'd tie his shoes if he had to.'

Or to criticize:

'I didn't make that up. I read it in a magazine.'
'**Magazine schmagazine**. It's complete garbage. Don't believe everything you read!'

2 **playfully:** spielerisch. | **to poke fun at s.th.:** sich über etwas lustig machen. | 3 **to deflate** (fig.): einen Dämpfer aufsetzen. | **pretension:** Anmaßung, Überheblichkeit. | 4 **fancy:** nobel, schick. | 8 **mononucleosis:** Pfeiffersches Drüsenfieber.

Or to make little of / diminish something:

'We can't drive in that snow.'
'**Snow schmow**. It'll just take us a little longer.'

'Joe Schmoe' is a reduplication of this kind that has become a fixed expression. It refers to any old guy.

'She finally got married.'
'Yeah, she was desperate. She married the first **Joe Schmoe** who proposed to her.'

Smash, Bang, Crash, Plop!

Don't miss the game on page 166 ff.

There is a very long word for words that sound like what they mean, such as *smash, bang* or *plop*: onomatopoeia. But who cares what they're called. Let's hear a few.

Fingernails **grate** on a blackboard.

An airplane propeller **whirs**.

A supersonic jet makes a sonic **boom**.

Walking on small stones makes a **crunching** sound.

Firecrackers go **bang**.

1 **to diminish:** (ver)mindern, verringern. | 8 **to propose to s.o.:** jdm. einen Heiratsantrag machen. | 12 **onomatopoeia** [ˌɒnəmætəˈpiːə]: Lautmalerei. | 16 **supersonic jet:** Überschallflugzeug. | 18 **firecracker:** Knallkörper.

A wheel that needs oil **squeaks**.

Loud ocean waves **roar**.

Water that slowly drops from a faucet **drips**.

Bacon frying in a pan **sizzles**.

If you open a champagne bottle, you hear a loud **pop**.

An apple **plops** off the tree into a pond below.

Tyres **screech** around a corner when you drive too fast.

If you drop a sack of flour on the floor, it makes a **thud**.

Water **gurgles** when you pour it out of a bottle.

People should **knock** on a door before going in.

Angry people **slam** the door.

A horse bothered by flies **swishes** its tail.

Before a storm, you can hear a **rumble** in the sky.

Babies like to shake a **rattle**.

When it is raining, you can hear the **patter** on the roof.

When a smith hammers metal, it goes **clang**.

Chain links make a **clanking** sound.

A kettle **hisses** when it makes steam.

Keys **jingle** on a key chain.

Tiny bells **tinkle**. Small bells **jingle**. Church bells **chime**.

17 **chain link:** Kettenglied.

Champagne glasses **clink**.

Dropping a tray of dishes makes a **clatter**.

When there is a car accident you hear a **crash**.

Soda **fizzes**.

Clocks and watches **tick**.

In a storm, a tree branch may **snap**.

A flag **flaps** in heavy wind.

Boiling water **bubbles**.

A fire **crackles**.

A baby **splashes** in a bathtub.

Fallen leaves **rustle** in the wind.

Whips **crack**.

Old doors **creak** when they're opened.

Bees **buzz** around a hive.

The water in a stream **burbles** as it flows by.

12 **whip:** Peitsche. | 14 **(bee)hive:** Bienenstock.

Cows Moo, Do You?

Animal language ... onomatopoeia:
Don't miss the game on page 166 ff.

Birds **chirp**.

Cats **meow**.

Chickens **cluck**.

Cows **low**.

Crickets **chirp**.

Crows **caw**.

Dogs **bark**.

Donkeys **bray**.

Ducks **quack**.

Elephants **trumpet**.

Flies **buzz**.

Frogs **croak**.

Geese **honk**.

Horses **whinney**.

Hyenas **laugh**.

Lions **roar**.

Mice **squeak**.

2 **onomatopoeia** [ˌɒnəmætəˈpiːə]: Lautmalerei. | 8 **cricket:** Grille.

Owls **hoot**.

Peacocks **scream**.

Pigs **grunt**.

Pigeons **coo**.

Roosters **crow**.

Sheep **bleat**.

Snakes **hiss**.

Turkeys **gobble**.

Wolves **howl**.

A mouse is in his mousehole and he wants to go out to look for something to eat, but he's afraid there might be a cat outside. He puts his ear by the opening and listens, but all he hears is 'bow wow'. 'Well,' he thinks, 'there can't be a cat out there because I can hear a dog barking.' So he leaves his mousehole – and is promptly caught and eaten by a cat, who licks his lips and says 'It's good to be bilingual.'

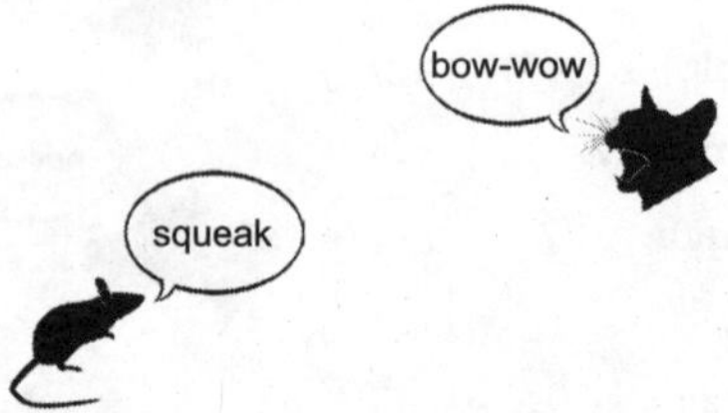

1 **owl:** Eule. | 2 **peacock:** Pfau. | 4 **pigeon** ['pɪdʒɪn]: Taube. | 5 **rooster:** Hahn.

Questionable Quotes

Things people have said that, well, don't make sense; things nobody has ever said that are funny anyway; crazy things people have actually written …

It's better to keep your mouth closed and let people think you are a fool than to open it and remove all doubt.
Mark Twain

Famous Last Words

When we say 'famous last words' we might think of a lion tamer whose last words were 'I thought you fed the lions this morning ...'; or the son of the U.S. President asking his father 'What's this red button for?' Or, to mention an historical example, General John Sedgwick, who was killed in 1864 during the U.S. Civil War at the battle of Spotsylvania. His last words, as he peeked over the hill to look towards the enemy, were:

'They couldn't hit an elephant at this distan...'

In the case of the rock musician Terry Kath, his last words were:

'Don't worry, it's not loaded.'

A postcard from somebody on holiday in Australia might read something like this:

Anyway, she ran into the water and shouted 'No crocodiles here!' Famous last words. A few moments later a large crocodile was having her for breakfast.

Here are some more 'famous last words'. Note they don't necessarily mean the speaker died.

Don't worry; that bear is sleeping.

Are you sure the power is off?

8 **to peek:** spähen, lugen.

Let it down slowly.

These are the 'good' mushrooms.

It's strong enough for both of us.

The odds of that happening have to be a million to one!

OK, I'll hold it and you light the fuse.

Don't worry, mum. I'll study for the exam tomorrow.

Famous People's Famous Last Words

These 'famous last words' were spoken by famous people just before they **croaked** (see p. 105) – and some of them might even be actual quotes.

It has all been very interesting.
Mary Wortley Montagu, 1762

So this is death – well …
Thomas Carlyle, 1881

One last drink, please.
Jack Daniel, 1911

If this is dying, then I don't think much of it.
Lytton Strachey, 1932

I wish I'd drunk more champagne.
John Maynard Keynes, 1946

4 **the odds** (pl.): die Chancen, die Wahrscheinlichkeit. | 5 **fuse:** Zündschnur. | 10 **actual:** hier: echt.

I've had eighteen straight whiskies, I think that's the record.
Dylan Thomas, 1953

Oh, I am so bored with it all.
Winston Churchill, 1965

Dying is a very dull, dreary affair. And my advice to you is to have nothing whatever to do with it.
W. Somerset Maugham, 1965

I'd hate to die twice. It's so boring.
Richard Feynman, American physicist, 1988

You can see that some people find dying quite boring. One way of making your death more interesting is to be executed. So, let's finish off our famous last words with some executions. Two of them involve the electric chair. In 1928 George Appel was convicted of murder for killing a police officer in New York City. Appel was sentenced to death by electric chair. While he was being strapped in to the chair he said:

"Well, gentlemen, you are about to see a baked Appel."

James French was the last man to be given the electric chair in the state of Oklahoma. He asked the officers as they strapped him in:

"How's this for a headline? 'French fries'."

1 **straight:** (Alkohol) pur. | 5 **dull:** öde, langweilig. | **dreary** ['drɪəri]: eintönig, öde. | 16 **to strap in:** festschnallen. | 17 **to be about to do s.th.:** im Begriff sein etwas zu tun. | 21 **French fries** (pl.): Pommes frites.

The murderer James W. Rodgers, finally, was executed by a firing squad in Utah in 1960. He was asked whether he had a final request. He said:

> "Why yes – a bullet-proof vest."

Bushisms

In Australia and New Zealand, bushisms are words used by people who live in the bush (out **woop-woop**, see p. 27). For example, they say 'tinned cow' instead of 'condensed milk'. But now a Bushism also refers to "a verbal peculiarity [...] associated with George W. Bush"[4]. In other words, Bushisms are stupid comments made by George W. Bush. Here is an example:

> "More and more of our imports come from overseas."

This is rubbish, of course, just like when he spoke of America as a "nation of more than 300 people". Obviously, George W. Bush is **not the sharpest knife in the drawer** (see p. 113), and sometimes he seemed to be out of touch with the modern world. He once mentioned "rumours on the internets", and he talked about using "the Google". A close advisor, Donald Rumsfeld, George W. Bush's Secretary of Defense, was also famous for his use of words. He was very good at saying simple things in complicated ways.

4 This is the definition according to the Oxford English Dictionary.

1f. **firing squad:** Erschießungskommando. | 14 **rubbish** (coll.): Quatsch. | 18 **rumour:** Gerücht.

George W. Bush is not the only politician in the family who has uttered such nonsense. His father, George H. W. Bush, once said "We have had triumphs, we have made mistakes; we have had sex". It even rubbed off on his Vice President, Dan Quayle, who came up with some **doozies** (see p. 14) himself.

Here is a collection of some of the best Bushisms, Quayleisms, and Rumsfeldisms.

George W. Bush

"Rarely is the question asked: is our children learning?"

"They misunderestimated me."

"I know the human being and fish can coexist peacefully."

"For every fatal shooting, there were roughly three non-fatal shootings. And, folks, this is unacceptable in America. It's just unacceptable. And we're going to do something about it."

"I think we agree. The past is over."

"You teach a child to read, and he or her will be able to pass a literacy test."

"A lot of times in politics you have people look you in the eye and tell you what's not on their mind."

"The best way to relieve families from time to time is to let them keep some of their own money."

2 **to utter:** von sich geben, äußern. | 4 **to rub off on s.o.** (fig.): auf jdn. abfärben. | 14 **folk(s):** Leute. | 18 **literacy test:** Lesetest.

"I understand small business growth. I was one."

"Will the highways on the Internet become more few?"

Dan Quayle

"The President is going to lead us out of this recovery."

"This election is about who is going to be the next President of the United States!"

"I feel this is my first year, that next year is an election year, that the third year is the mid-point, and that the fourth year is the last chance I'll have to make a record since the last two years."

"I have made good judgements in the past. I have made good judgements in the future."

"My friends, no matter how rough the road may be, we can and we will, never, never surrender to what is right."

"If we do not succeed, then we run the risk of failure."

"We are ready for any unforeseen event that may or may not occur."

"I believe we are on an irreversible trend toward more freedom and democracy – but that could change."

"One word sums up probably the responsibility of any Vice President, and that one word is 'to be prepared'."

9 **record:** hier etwa: Vermächtnis.

"Welcome to President Bush, Mrs. Bush, and my fellow astronauts."

"I stand by all the misstatements that I've made."

Donald Rumsfeld

As Secretary of Defense, Rumsfeld was not a fool, but he was well known for **bloviating** (see p. 13), as shown below. Can you make sense of this?

> "Reports that say that something hasn't happened are always interesting to me, because as we know, there are known knowns; there are things we know we know. We also know there are known unknowns; that is to say we know there are some things we do not know. But there are also unknown unknowns – the ones we don't know we don't know."
>
> "I believe what I said yesterday. I don't know what I said, but I know what I think, and, well, I assume it's what I said."

More Crazy Things People Have Said

It is, of course, completely unfair to pick on Bush, Quayle and Rumsfeld. Throughout history, people have been saying things that are, well, nonsensical.

1 f. **fellow astronaut:** etwa: Mitastronaut. | 3 **to stand by s.th.:** zu etwas stehen. | 17 **to pick on s.o.:** auf jdm. herumhacken; hier: jdn. aussuchen.

Samuel Goldwyn (1882–1974) was born in Poland and emigrated to the U. S. where he became a Hollywood film producer. He is well-remembered for mangling English. Here are a few of his more memorable comments.

"I never liked you, and I always will."

"If I could drop dead right now, I'd be the happiest man alive."

"Nobody should write his autobiography until after he's dead."

"Don't talk to me while I'm interrupting."

"Go see it and see for yourself why you shouldn't see it."

"A verbal contract isn't worth the paper it's written on."

"If he was alive today, he'd be turning over in his grave."

"We have all passed a lot of water since then."

"Coffee isn't my cup of tea."

"When I want your opinion, I'll give it to you."

Yogi Berra was an American Major League baseball player and manager. Like Goldwyn, he became well known for his unique way of twisting logic.

"Baseball is ninety per cent mental and the other half is physical."

3 **to mangle:** radebrechen. | 4 **memorable:** denkwürdig; einprägsam. | 15 **not my cup of tea** (fig.): nicht mein Ding. | 18 **unique** [juːˈniːk]: einzigartig, einmalig.

"The future ain't what it used to be."

"In theory there is no difference between theory and practice. In practice there is."

"No wonder nobody comes here – it's too crowded."

"Always go to other people's funerals: otherwise they won't come to yours."

"I never said most of the things I said."

Here are a few others by unknown speakers …

"The climate of the Sahara means that its inhabitants have to live elsewhere."

"If I did say that, I was misquoted."

"Most dreams are about everyday things – falling, flying, walking naked down the street."

Headlines

Newspapers often get it wrong, too. Writing a headline can be a very tricky business. You don't have much space, you don't have much time, and you're not allowed to use those useful little words 'the', 'a' and 'an'. The results can be very funny, and sometimes a little grotesque.

PARAMEDICS HELP SPIDER BITE VICTIM

20 **paramedic:** Sanitäter(in).

MAN DIES AFTER SUICIDE ATTEMPT

BRITISH LEFT WAFFLES ON FALKLAND ISLANDS

LAWYERS GIVE POOR LEGAL ADVICE

NURSES NEEDED TO HELP STROKE PATIENTS

VICE-CHANCELLOR TO STOP DRINKING ON CAMPUS

SEX MORE COMMON THAN THOUGHT

MARCH PLANNED FOR APRIL

QUEEN MARY HAVING BOTTOM SCRAPED

VIAGRA STOLEN. POLICE SEEK HARDENED CRIMINALS

SCIENTISTS TO HAVE OBAMA'S EAR

PROSTITUTES APPEAL TO POPE

PANDA MATING FAILS: VETERINARIAN TAKES OVER

EYE DROPS OFF SHELF

STOLEN PAINTING FOUND BY TREE

1 **waffle:** (Nomen) Waffel; (Verb) schwafeln. | 7 **Queen Mary: 1.** Maria von Teck (1867–1953); englische Königin; **2.** Passagierschiff. | **bottom: 1.** Unterseite; **2.** Hintern. | **to scrape:** ab-, auskratzen, schaben. | 8 **hardened criminal:** Gewohnheitsverbrecher(in). | 11 **mating:** Paarung. | 12 **shelf:** Regal(brett).

Bumper Stickers

If you're stuck in a traffic jam and in a bad mood, a bumper sticker on the car in front of you might brighten up your day …

If you can read this, I've lost my caravan.

If you don't like the way I drive, get off the sidewalk!

As a matter of fact, I **do** own the road.

Sometimes drivers are making fun of themselves:

My wife keeps complaining I never listen to her … or something like that.

I married my wife for her looks … but not the ones she's been giving me lately!

Seen it all, done it all, can't remember most of it.

Some bumper stickers are questions:

Why be difficult when you can be impossible?

What's another word for Thesaurus?

Is a castrated pig disgruntled?

Why is it that most nudists are people you don't want to see naked?

1 **bumper sticker:** Autoaufkleber. | 16 **disgruntled:** verärgert, verstimmt. Wortspiel mit *to grunt:* grunzen.

Some offer words of wisdom or food for thought:

The more people I meet, the more I like my dog.

A woman without a man is like a fish without a bicycle.

Change is inevitable, except from a vending machine.

Always remember you're unique, just like everyone else.

Procrastinators Unite! … Tomorrow.

Some make fun of famous quotes or everyday language. Do you know what these bumper stickers refer to?

(1) Warning: Dates in calendar are closer than they appear.

(2) Give me ambiguity or give me something else.

(3) When all else fails, manipulate the data.

(4) Make beer not war.

(5) I don't have a license to kill. I have a learner's permit.

(6) Boldly Going Nowhere.

(7) You have the right to remain silent. Anything you say will be misquoted, then used against you.

(1) 'Objects in mirror are closer than they appear' – warning on car door mirrors in the U. S. and Canada.

1 **wisdom:** Weisheit. | 4 **inevitable** [ɪ'nevɪtəbəl]: unvermeidlich. | **vending machine:** (Münz-, Waren-)Automat. | 5 **unique** [juː'niːk]: einzigartig, einmalig. | 6 **procrastinator:** Zögerer/Zögerin, Zauderer/Zauderin. | 10 **ambiguity:** Doppel-, Mehrdeutigkeit. | 14 **boldly:** mutig, kühn.

(2) “Give me liberty or give me death” – Patrick Henry, Governor of Virginia, before the War of American Independence.

(3) ‘If everything else fails, read the instructions’ (see p. 55).

(4) ‘Make love, not war’ was a slogan of the peace movement in the late 1960s.

(5) James Bond has a ‘license to kill’; new drivers get a ‘learner’s permit’.

(6) The U.S. cult series *Star Trek* begins with a quote about the crew’s mission ‘to boldly go where no man has gone before.’

(7) U.S. police officers read the ‘Miranda rights’ to anybody they arrest: ‘You have the right to remain silent. Anything you say can and will be used against you in a court of law.’

Silly Signage

In a restaurant: If you don’t like our waiters, you should see the manager.

In a laundromat: Remove all clothing before leaving.

On a highway: When this sign is under water, this road is closed.

Outside a school: No trespassing without permission.

Outside a clinic: Hours 9:00–5:00. Emergencies only after hours.

13 **signage** ['saɪnɪdʒ]: Beschilderung, Ausschilderung. | 16 **laundromat:** Waschsalon. | 19 **trespassing:** unbefugtes Betreten. | 20 f. **after hours:** außerhalb der Öffnungszeiten.

Outside a maternity ward: No children allowed.

At a military base: Restricted to unauthorized personnel.

Toilet closed for repairs. Please use the floor below.

On a church bulletin board: On Easter Sunday, we will ask Mrs. J. to come forward and lay an egg on the altar.

Classified Ads

Dog for sale: Eats everything and likes children.

For sale: antique desk suitable for lady with thick legs.

Tired of cleaning yourself? Let me do it.

Stock up and save. Limit: one.

Cottage, 2 bedrooms, lounge, kitchen, bathroom, separate WC occupied until end of month.

Vacation special: Have your home exterminated.

Toaster: A gift that every member of the family appreciates. Automatically burns toast.

Used cars: Why go elsewhere to be cheated? Come here first!

Sandwich Special Turkey $ 5.50, Chicken or Beef $ 5.25; Children $ 2.50.

1 **maternity ward:** Entbindungsstation. | 4 **bulletin** ['bʊlətɪn] **board:** schwarzes Brett. | 6 **classified ad:** Kleinanzeige. | 10 **to stock up:** sich eindecken, Vorräte anlegen. | 13 **to exterminate:** ausrotten, vernichten (*exterminator:* Kammerjäger).

Wanted: Man to take care of cow that does not smoke or drink.

Illiterate? Write today for free help.

Semi-annual after-Christmas sale.

Auto Repair Service. Free pick-up and delivery. Try us once, you'll never go anywhere again.

Ad for a gas station: Eat here and get gas.

Church Bulletin Typos

Rent-a-man. Weeknights or weekends, any and all types of work. I even do widows.

Babysitter wanted. Peasant working conditions.

Wanted: someone to change the church nursery sheets and wash the dirty ones each wee.

Choir rehearsal will be hell as usual on Wednesday night.

Alcoholics Anonymous – were here to help you.

2 **illiterate** [ɪ'lɪtərɪt]: des Lesens und Schreibens unkundig. | 7 **church bulletin** ['bʊlətɪn]: Gemeindebrief. | **typo:** Druckfehler. | 10 **peasant** ['pezənt]: bäuerlich. | 12 **wee** (coll.): Pipi.

Accident Reports

It can be very difficult to describe a traumatic event clearly in the limited space given on the form …

An invisible car came out of nowhere, hit my vehicle, and vanished.

The guy was all over the road. I had to swerve a number of times before I hit him.

Coming home, I drove into the wrong house and collided with a tree I don't have.

The pedestrian had no idea which direction to go, so I ran over him.

I had been driving my car for forty years when I fell asleep at the wheel and had an accident.

A pedestrian hit me and went under my car.

The car in front hit the pedestrian but he got up so I hit him again.

I collided with a parked truck coming the other way.

I thought my window was down, but I found it was up when I put my head through it.

I had been learning to drive with power steering. I turned the wheel to what I thought was enough and found myself in a different direction going the opposite way.

My car was legally parked as it backed into the other vehicle.

6 **to swerve:** (Auto) plötzlich ausweichen. | 20 **power steering:** Servolenkung.

I was sure the old fellow would never make it to the other side of the road when I struck him.

Company Condoms

It's high time that major companies started producing – or at least sponsoring – condoms. Combined with their mottos, they would make great advertising campaigns.

Nike Condoms: *Just do it.*

Toyota Condoms: *Oh what a feeling!*

Microsoft Condoms: *Where do you want to go today?*

KFC Condoms: *Finger licking good.*

M&Ms Condoms: *Melt in your mouth, not in your hands.*

McDonald's Condoms: *I'm lovin' it.*

Ford Condoms: *Feel the difference.*

Energizer Condoms: *Keep going and going and going.*

Pringles Condoms: *Once you pop, you can't stop.*

Goodyear Condoms: *Made to feel good.*

BMW Condoms: *Pure driving pleasure.*

Nutella Condoms: *Breakfast never tasted this good.*

Burger King Condoms: *Have it your way.*

1 **old fellow:** alter Knabe. | 10 **KFC:** *Kentucky Fried Chicken* (US-amerikanische Fast-Food-Kette).

Pearls of Wisdom

Throughout our lives, we are confronted with difficult situations. But we are not alone. These authors have given these difficulties some thought.

The single biggest problem in communication is the illusion that it has taken place.
George Bernard Shaw

An egotist is a person more interested in himself than in me.
Ambrose Bierce

If everything seems to be going well, you have obviously overlooked something.
Steven Wright

Just because you're paranoid don't mean they're not after you.
Kurt Cobain

I know that you believe you understand what you think I said, but I'm not sure you realize that what you heard is not what I meant.
Robert McCloskey

Friends come and go, but enemies accumulate.
Thomas Jones

There is so little difference between husbands, you might as well keep the first.
Adela Rogers St. Johns

1 **wisdom:** Weisheit. | 13 f. **to be after s.o.:** hinter jdm. her sein, jdn. verfolgen.

I am not young enough to know everything.
Oscar Wilde

Always be sincere, even when you don't mean it.
Irene Peter

It ain't over till it's over!
Yogi Berra

Everything I like is either illegal, immoral or fattening.
Alexander Woollcott

If everything else fails, read the instructions.
Ralph Waldo Emerson

From a few unknown authors:

The ability to speak several languages is an asset, but the ability to keep your mouth shut in any language is priceless.

There are three little words that can save a marriage: you're right, dear.

Experience teaches you to recognize a mistake when you've made it again.

The qualities that most attract a woman to a man are usually the same ones she can't stand years later.

3 **sincere:** aufrichtig, ehrlich. | 12 **asset:** Vorteil, Pluspunkt.

Murphy's Law

Nobody really knows where Murphy's law came from. According to one theory it is named after Captain Edward A. Murphy, who did experiments for the U.S. Air Force in 1949 and found problems everywhere.

In its simplest form, Murphy's law states that:

Anything that can go wrong will go wrong.

Here are some examples of this law:

The other line always moves faster.

Anything you fix will take longer and cost more than you thought.

The repairman will never have seen a model quite like yours before.

In order to get a loan, you must first prove you don't need it.

No matter how long or hard you shop for an item, as soon as you've bought it, it will be on sale somewhere cheaper.

The light at the end of the tunnel is the headlamp of an oncoming train.

The chance of a piece of bread falling with the buttered side down is directly proportional to the cost of the carpet.

17 **headlamp:** Scheinwerfer. | 17 f. **oncoming:** entgegenkommend.

Translations and Other Misunderstandings

Communication is difficult even when people speak the same language. Add several languages to the equation and it can be a recipe for disaster – or for laughter.

Translation is a difficult art.
Übersetzung ist eine schwierige Kunst.
La traduction est un art difficile.
Tərcümə çətin sənətdir.
예술을 번역하기 어려운
Anodd i gyfieithu'r celf.
لکشم ےئل ےک ےنرک ہمجرت نف
Nehéz lefordítani művészet.
لکشم ےئل ےک ےنرک ہمجرت نف
Anodd i gyfieithu celf.
예술을 번역하기 어려운
Incəsənət tərcümə çətinlik çəkirəm.
J'ai du mal à interpréter l'art.
Ich finde es schwer zu interpretieren Kunst.
I find it difficult to interpret art.[5]

5 Courtesy of Google Translator: English, German, French, Azerbaijani, Korean, Welsh, Urdu, Hungarian and back again.

4 **equation:** Gleichung.

Helpful Information for English-Speaking Tourists ...

Hotels

Tokyo: Is forbitten to steal hotel towels please. If you are not person to do such thing is please not to read notice.

Athens: Visitors are expected to complain at the office between the hours of 9 and 11 a. m. daily.

Innsbruck: Not to perambulate the corridors in the hours of repose in the boots of ascension.

Paris: You are invited to take advantage of the chambermaid.

Zurich: Because of the impropriety of entertaining guests of the opposite sex in the bedroom, it is suggested that the lobby be used for this purpose.

Bucharest: The lift is being fixed for the next day. During that time we regret that you will be unbearable.

Nice: Please leave your values at the front desk.

8 **to perambulate** (form.): spazierengehen. | 8 f. **repose:** Ruhe. | 9 **ascension:** Aufstieg; (Christi) Himmelfahrt. | 10 **to take advantage of s.o.:** jdn. (meist sexuell) ausnutzen. | **chambermaid:** Zimmermädchen. | 11 **impropriety:** Unschicklichkeit. | 15 **unbearable:** unerträglich. | 16 **Nice** [niːs]: Nizza.

Restaurant Menus

Bern: Special today: No ice cream.

Zagreb: Our wines leave nothing to hope for.

Leipzig: We only serve free running brown eggs.

Warsaw: Salad a firm's own make limpid red beet soup with cheesy dumplings in the form of a finger; roasted duck let loose; beef rashers beaten up in the country people's fashion.

Kyoto: Special cocktails for ladies with nuts.

Oslo: Ladies are requested not to have children in the bar.

Shops

In a Hong Kong supermarket: For your convenience, we recommend polite, efficient self-service.

Outside a Hong Kong tailor shop: Ladies may have a fit upstairs.

In a Bangkok dry cleaner's: Drop your trousers here for best results.

Outside a Paris dress shop: Dresses for street walking.

In a Rhodes tailor shop: Order your summer suit. Because is a big rush we will execute customers in strict rotation.

5 **limpid:** klar, durchsichtig. | **red beet:** Rote Rübe. | 6 **dumpling:** Knödel, Kloß. | 7 **rasher:** Speckscheibe. | 8 **nuts: 1.** Nüsse; **2.** (sl.) Eier (Hoden). | 11 **convenience:** Annehmlichkeit. | 16 **street walking:** *streetwalking* (coll.): Straßenstrich. | 17 **Rhodes:** Rhodos. | 18 **to execute s.o.:** jdn. hinrichten (*to execute s.th.:* etwas ausführen).

In a Chinatown pet shop: Buy one dog, get one flee.

In a Rome laundry: Ladies, leave your clothes here and spend the afternoon having a good time.

Miscellaneous

A sign from the Black Forest: It is strictly forbidden on our Black Forest camping site that people of different sex, for instance men and women, live together in one tent unless they are married with each other for that purpose.

Advertisement for donkey rides in Thailand: Would you like to ride on your own ass?

On the faucet in a Finnish washroom: To stop the drip, turn cock to right.

At a Budapest zoo: Please do not feed the animals. If you have any suitable food, give it to the guard on duty.

Detour sign in Kyushi, Japan: Stop: Drive Sideways.

In a Bangkok temple: It is forbidden to enter a woman, even a foreigner, if dressed as a man.

In a Copenhagen airline ticket office: We take your bags and send them in all directions.

1 **flee:** *flea:* Floh. | 4 **miscellaneous** [ˌmɪsəˈleɪnɪəs]: Sonstiges, Verschiedenes. | 10 **ass: 1.** (Tier) Esel; **2.** (BE, coll.) Esel, Dummkopf; **3.** (AE, sl.) Arsch. | 11 **drip:** (Geräusch) Tropfen. | 12 **cock: 1.** Gockel, Hahn; **2.** (Absperr-)Hahn; **3.** (vulg.) Pimmel, Schwanz. | 14 **on duty:** diensthabend, im Dienst. | 15 **sideways:** seitwärts. | 16 **to enter s.o.:** (Geschlechtsverkehr) in jdn. eindringen.

From the brochure of a car rental firm in Tokyo: When passenger of foot heave in sight, tootle the horn. Trumpet him melodiously at first, but if he still obstacles your passage then tootle him with vigour.

In the office of a Roman doctor: Specialist in women and other diseases.

F---ing Kinky

Have you heard of the Austrian village Fucking? You probably have, because the residents of Fucking regularly complain about tourists who come to Fucking to steal the town's sign.

The Japanese district Kinki had a similar problem. *Kinky*, in case you didn't know, means unconventional, strange or bizarre – especially in the sexual sense. When this was brought to the attention of the Kinki residents, company names, such as the 'Kinki Research Complex', 'Kinki Nippon Tourist', and the English-language tourist magazine *Kinki*, suddenly seemed embarrassing. The officials of Kinki decided something had to be done, and Kinki was replaced with Kansai.

While the Kinki Japanese gave in to the global language English, the residents of Fucking have not. They are adamantly resisting. As the Mayor of Fucking recently said: "For us, Fucking is Fucking – and it's going to stay Fucking."[6]

6 Haywood, Anthony; Walker, Kerry, *Lonely Planet. Austria* (5th ed.), 2008, p. 217.

2 **to tootle:** dudeln; hier: hupen. | 3 **obstacle:** Hindernis (*to be an obstacle:* behindern). | 4 **vigour:** Kraft, Vitalität; Nachdruck. | 20 **adamantly** ['ædəməntlı]: hartnäckig.

Marketing Troubles

Sometimes advertisers go to great trouble to translate their slogans into another language with the aim of drawing attention to their product overseas. This is not always a good idea, as can be seen from the following examples:

Beer Brewer Coors translated its slogan, 'Turn It Loose', into Spanish, where it was read as 'Suffer From Diarrhoea'.

The American chicken magnate Frank Purdue's slogan 'It takes a tough man to make a tender chicken,'[7] sounds much more interesting in Spanish: 'It takes a sexually stimulated man to make a chicken affectionate.'

When Pepsi started marketing its products in China, they translated their slogan 'Pepsi Brings You Back to Life' figuratively. The slogan in Chinese actually meant, 'Pepsi Brings Your Ancestors Back from the Grave.'

When Coca-Cola first shipped to China, they named the product something that when pronounced sounded like 'Coca-Cola'. The only problem was that the characters used meant 'bite the wax tadpole'. They later used a set of characters that mean 'happiness in the mouth'.

An American T-shirt maker in Miami printed shirts for the Spanish market which promoted the Pope's visit. Instead of 'I saw the Pope' (el Papa), the shirts read 'I saw the potato' (la papa).

7 Purdue thought himself 'tough' because the regulations he used to maintain the quality of his chickens were stricter (tougher) than the legal standards.

3 **to draw attention to s.th.:** die Aufmerksamkeit auf etwas lenken. |
19 **tadpole:** Kaulquappe.

Sometimes it's not the slogan that's the problem, but rather the product itself:

> Have you ever wondered why the Mitsubishi 'Pajero' is known as the 'Montero' in the U.S.? 'Pajero' in Spanish means 'wanker'.
>
> The Chevy Nova never sold well in Spanish-speaking countries. Maybe because 'No Va' means 'It does not go' in Spanish.
>
> Clairol tried to introduce the 'Mist Stick', a curling iron, in Germany, but no one had use for a 'manure stick'.
>
> Scandinavian vacuum manufacturer Electrolux quickly stopped using their slogan in America: 'Nothing sucks like an Electrolux.'
>
> And the American tissue manufacturer, Puffs, was simply unsuccessful introducing any of their products in Germany …

The Germans themselves, however, are to be congratulated for the way they use English to make their products sound more appealing. After all, they have created one of the best names for toilet paper anywhere: 'Happy End Toilettenpapier'. German dog owners, however, who want only the best for their pets and buy raw food to feed them, might consider a different term than BARF (**B**orn **A**gain **R**aw **F**eeders; see p. 110) when referring to themselves.

5 **wanker** (vulg.): Wichser. | 10 **manure** [məˈnjʊə]: Dung, Mist. | 12 **to suck** (AE, coll.): ätzend/Scheiße sein.

Colourful Language

What is more fun than a barrel of monkeys? English has more idioms than you can shake a stick at. And collective nouns out the wazoo (see p. 17). A school of fish, a flock of birds … What would you call a group of Australians?

As blind as a bat.

Colours

Children colour in pictures in colouring books. A good walk on a crisp autumn morning puts colour in your cheeks. Painting the walls in a house adds some colour to the decor. But what about adding a little colour to your life? Don't be yellow (afraid). Are you green with envy or feeling blue? (Sad, not drunk!) Is your company in the red? Or in the black? Are you feeling in the pink (very well)? There is a big grey area that's hard to define! I don't feel like repeating myself until I'm blue in the face, but colour can spice up your language. One way to do that is to sprinkle in some idioms!

Colour Your World with Idioms

Idioms reflect day-to-day life, including cooking, eating, work and sport. Idioms about the human body are particularly common. In fact, there are hundreds of them. Don't roll your eyes, it's true!

Don't miss the games on page 165.

Sometimes German and English speakers see the world in a similar way …

on the tip of your tongue liegt mir auf der Zunge
to roll your eyes die Augen verdrehen

2 **to colour in s.th.:** etwas anmalen/ausmalen. | 3 **crisp:** (Luft) frisch. | 10 **to spice up:** mehr Würze verleihen, aufpeppen. | 11 **to sprinkle in:** einstreuen.

to have someone eating out of the palm of your hand jemand frisst dir aus der Hand
to have balls Eier haben
to give someone the cold shoulder jemandem die kalte Schulter zeigen
to shoot from the hip aus der Hüfte schießen
to talk someone's ear off jemandem ein Ohr abkauen
to have a mind like a sieve ein Gedächtnis wie ein Sieb haben
to pull/tear your hair out over something sich die Haare ausraufen über etwas
racking your brains sich den Kopf zerbrechen
wet behind the ears feucht hinter den Ohren
to turn a blind eye bei etwas ein Auge zudrücken

But they don't always see things in quite the same way …

to laugh your head off sich totlachen
two-faced doppelzüngig
neck and neck Kopf an Kopf
two heads are better than one vier Augen sehen mehr als zwei
you scratch my back and I'll scratch yours eine Hand wäscht die andere
thick-skinned ein dickes Fell haben
to cross your fingers die Daumen drücken
to have two left feet zwei linke Hände haben

And sometimes they have completely different imaginations …

to get your nose bent out of shape eine beleidigte Leberwurst sein

to stick your foot in your mouth ins Fettnäpfchen treten
to know something/somewhere like the back of your hand etwas wie seine Westentasche kennen
to leg it die Beine in die Hand nehmen
to have a bone to pick with someone mit jemandem ein Hühnchen rupfen
a pain in the neck eine Nervensäge
to keep a stiff upper lip die Ohren steifhalten
to pull someone's leg jemanden auf den Arm nehmen
to be on its last legs aus dem letzten Loch pfeifen
to shoot yourself in the foot sich ins Knie schießen
to stick your neck out for someone sich für jemanden aus dem Fenster lehnen
to have a millstone around your neck einen Klotz am Bein haben
to stick out like a sore thumb auffallen wie ein bunter Hund
to escape by the skin of your teeth um Haaresbreite davonkommen

We Don't See Eye to Eye!?

Sometimes English and German speakers simply do NOT see 'eye to eye' about the world, and then idioms are just not translatable. In these cases, there is just no equivalent expression in German – oder haben Sie schon mal jemandem das haarige Auge gegeben? A picture is worth a thousand words …

21 f. **to see eye to eye:** übereinstimmen. | 23 **equivalent** [ɪ'kwɪvələnt]: gleichwertig, entsprechend.

to give someone the hairy eyeball a look of suspicion or hostility. *When he forgot their anniversary, she gave him the hairy eyeball.*

to be tongue-tied to be speechless, usually due to embarrassment. *When he asked her why she wouldn't marry him, she was tongue-tied.*

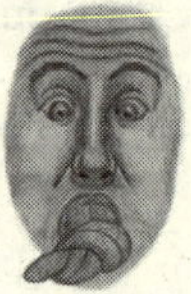

to crane your neck to stretch your neck in order to see or hear something better. *During the test he craned his neck to see his neighbour's anwers.*

to cost an arm and a leg to be very expensive. *Flying first class costs an arm and a leg.*

Don't Get Your Knickers in a Twist!

English speakers also enjoy using descriptive idioms using clothing …

to fly by the seat of your pants intuitiv handeln
to treat someone with kid gloves jemanden wie ein rohes Ei behandeln
don't get your knickers in a twist! mach kein Theater!
to get caught with your pants down to be caught in an embarrassing position (jemanden kalt erwischen)

Drunk As a Skunk? No. Sick As a Dog!

English uses a variety of animals to describe human characteristics. Most are easy to imagine, such as 'as quiet as a mouse', or 'as busy as a bee', but others are not intuitive at all, including 'happy as a clam' or 'sick as a dog', or 'silly as a goose'.

How would you describe yourself?
Maybe …

as **angry** … as a hornet

as **blind** … as a bat

as **busy** … as a bee/beaver

20 **hornet:** Hornisse. | 21 **bat:** Fledermaus. | 22 **beaver:** Biber.

as **crazy** … as a coot

as **cunning** … as a fox (BE)

as **drunk** … as a skunk

as **free** … as a bird

as **gentle** … as a lamb

as **hairy** … as a gorilla

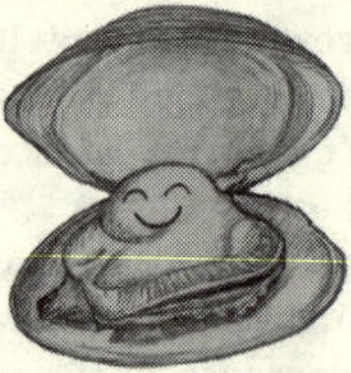

as **happy** … as a clam (AE)

as **playful** … as a kitten

as **poor** … as a church mouse

as **proud** … as a peacock

as **quiet** … as a mouse

as **sick** … as a dog

as **silly** … as a goose

as **slippery** … as an eel

as **sly** … as a fox (AE)

as **strong** … as an ox

as **stubborn** … as a mule

as **tall** … as a giraffe

as **timid** … as a rabbit

as **wise** … as an owl

1 **coot:** Wasserhuhn. | 2 **cunning:** schlau, gerissen. | 7 **clam:** Venusmuschel. | 8 **playful:** munter, verspielt. | **kitten:** Kätzchen. | 10 **peacock:** Pfau. | 14 **eel:** Aal. | 17 **stubborn** ['stʌbən]: störrisch. | **mule:** Maultier, Maulesel. | 19 **timid:** schüchtern; hier: furchtsam, scheu. | 20 **owl:** Eule.

Welches Tier gehört zu dir?

Using an animal's name directly can have a similar meaning to the comparison. For example, if someone is 'a mouse' then they are shy (which is similar to 'as quiet as a mouse'). But don't be fooled, calling someone a 'fox' means you think they are sexy (not cunning) and calling someone a dog means you think they're ugly (not sick). See how many of these you know.

Are you ...?

an **ass** (jerk)

a **chicken** (coward)

a **clam** (reticent, not talkative)

a **dog** (ugly)

a **fox** (sexy)

a **mouse** (shy)

a **pig** (slob)

a **skunk** (See **snake**.)

a **slug** (very slow)

a **snake** (dishonest)

a **teddybear** (cuddly)

4f. **don't be fooled:** lass dich / lassen Sie sich nicht täuschen. | 6 **cunning:** schlau, gerissen. | 9 **ass:** Esel. | **jerk:** Idiot. | 11 **clam:** Venusmuschel. | **reticent:** zurückhaltend. | **talkative:** gesprächig, redselig. | 15 **slob** (BE, coll.): Schlamper(in). | 17 **slug:** Nacktschnecke. | 19 **cuddly:** knuddelig.

a **weasel** (two-faced and sneaky)

a **whale** (obese)

a **worm** (a weasel, but worse)

Animal Idioms

Dogs and cats are particularly common in idioms …

to stick out like a dog's balls very noticeable. (See also **stick out like a sore thumb**, p. 69.)
to look like a dog's breakfast a complete mess. (See also **hodgepodge**, p. 25.)
to work like a dog to work hard
to bark up the wrong tree to make a false assumption and act on it (auf dem Holzweg sein)
to hound someone to pester someone to do something
to be in the doghouse to be on someone's shit list. *After he forgot her birthday he was in the doghouse until she forgave him.*

1 **two-faced:** heuchlerisch, falsch. | **sneaky:** gewieft; hinterhältig. | 2 **obese** [əʊ'biːs]: fett. | 13 **to pester s.o. to do s.th.:** jdn. bedrängen etwas zu tun. | 14 **shit list** (AE, vulg.): schwarze Liste.

to look like something the cat dragged in to look terrible. *After partying all night he looked like something the cat dragged in.*

a sheepish grin a smile when you get caught doing something embarrassing. *When she caught her son taking a cookie from the cookie jar, he gave her a sheepish grin.*

to open a can of worms to bring up a messy subject. *Talking about her mother-in-law was always like opening a can of worms.*

And a few others …

to pig out to eat way too much
to be an eager beaver a very enthusiastic person
to feel lousy to feel under the weather, to feel unwell
to be so hungry you could eat a horse famished, starving

8 **messy** (fig.): unschön, schwierig. | 12 **way too much** (coll.): viel zu viel. | 13 **beaver:** Biber. | 14 **to feel under the weather:** angeschlagen sein. | 15 **famished:** ausgehungert.

Collective Nouns

More Fun Than a Barrel of Monkeys!

Some animals move in groups and these groups have special names that range from common (a herd of cattle) and imaginative (a cloud of bats) to wildly creative (an ostentation of peacocks) or even ridiculous (an implausibility of gnus).

Most common:

Don't miss the game on page 169.

a **band** … of gorillas

a **bed** … of clams/oysters

a **caravan** … of camels

a **colony** … of ants

a **flock** … of sheep

a **flock** … of birds

a **herd** … of cattle

a **litter** … of kittens/puppies

a **mob** … of kangaroos

a **nest** … of mice

a **pack** … of wolves

a **pod** … of whales

4f. **to range from … to:** gehen/reichen von … bis. | 5f. **peacock:** Pfau. | 10 **clam:** Venusmuschel. | **oyster:** Auster. | 16 **kitten:** Kätzchen. | **puppy:** (Hunde-)Welpe.

a **pride** … of lions

a **school** … of fish

a **swarm** … of bees

a **troop** … of monkeys

Most creative:

an **ambush** … of tigers

a **bloat** … of hippopotamuses

a **business** … of ferrets

a **cackle** … of hyenas

a **cloud** … of bats

a **clowder** … of cats

a **cluster** … of spiders

a **crash** … of rhinoceroses

a **flight** … of dragons

a **fluther** … of jellyfish

6 **ambush:** Überfall aus dem Hinterhalt; hier (fig.): Rudel. Auch im folgenden handelt es sich um metaphorische Gruppenbezeichnungen mit diesen Grundbedeutungen: *bloat:* Blähung; *cackle:* meckerndes Lachen; *clowder:* Durcheinander; *implausibility:* Unglaubwürdigkeit; *infestation:* Heimsuchung; *ostentation:* Zurschaustellung, Prahlerei; *rabble:* lärmende Menge; *scold:* zänkisches Weib; *scurry:* Hoppeln, Trippeln; *shrewdness:* Gewitztheit, Klugheit. | 8 **ferret:** Frettchen. | 10 **bat:** Fledermaus. | 14 **dragon:** Drachen. | 15 **fluther of jellyfish:** Quallenschwarm.

an **implausibility** ... of gnus

an **infestation** ... of lice/fleas

a **knot** ... of toads

a **mess** ... of iguanas

a **murder** ... of crows

a **nest** ... of snakes

an **ostentation** ... of peacocks

a **parliament** ... of owls

a **passel** ... of possums

a **rabble** ... of buzzards

a **richness** ... of martens

a **scold** ... of jays

a **scurry** ... of squirrels

a **shrewdness** ... of apes

a **stand** ... of flamingos

a **watch** ... of nightingales

2 **louse** (pl. *lice*): Laus. | **flea:** Floh. | 3 **toad:** Kröte. | 4 **iguana** [ɪˈgwɑːnə]: Leguan. | 7 **peacock:** Pfau. | 8 **owl:** Eule. | 9 **passel of possums:** Beutelrattenschar. | 11 **marten:** Marder. | 12 **jay:** Eichelhäher. | 13 **squirrel:** Eichhörnchen. | 14 **ape:** Affe.

Just Ask the Board of Directors ...

Don't miss the game on page 169.

Just as animals move in groups, so do people. When a lot of people move together in one direction, we call them a 'throng of people'. Some of these collective nouns are very common (a crowd of people, a mob of angry protesters, a bunch of idiots), while others are not (a bevy of beauties, a den of thieves, a posse of deputies).

a **bench** ... of judges

a **bevy** ... of beauties

a **board** ... of directors

a **bunch** ... of idiots

a **busload** ... of tourists

a **choir** ... of singers

a **company** ... of actors

a **congregation** ... of churchgoers

a **coven** ... of witches

a **crowd** ... of people

a **den** ... of thieves

a **gaggle** ... of giggling girls

a **gang** ... of street kids

10 **bevy:** Schar, Schwarm. | 17 **coven:** (Hexen-)Zirkel. | 19 **den:** Höhle, Verschlag. | 20 **gaggle:** Schar. | **to giggle:** kichern.

a **host** ... of angels

a **mob** ... of angry protesters

a **pack** ... of thieves/liars

a **posse** ... of deputies

a **squadron** ... of pilots

a **staff** ... of assistants

a **team** ... of athletes

a **troop** ... of Boy Scouts

a **troupe** ... of dancers

Newly-coined collective nouns:[8]

a **call centre** ... of Indians

a **diaspora** ... of South Africans

a **drunkenness** ... of Irishmen

a **loudness** ... of Americans

a **miserliness** ... of Scotsman

a **melody** ... of Welshmen

a **pomposity** ... of Englishmen

8 These are possibly inventions of the editors.

1 **host:** Schar. | 4 **posse** ['pɒsi] (coll.): Gruppe. | 5 **squadron:** Staffel, Geschwader. | 10 **newly-coined:** (Wort) neugeschöpft, neugeprägt. | 15 **miserliness:** Geiz. | 16 **welshman:** Walliser. | 17 **pomposity:** Prunk, Pomp; hier: Blasiertheit, Wichtigtuerei.

a **quaintness** ... of New Zealanders

a **vulgarity** ... of Australians

a **wilderness** ... of Canadians

and finally ...

a **stiffness** ... of Germans

Tidbits

Did you know that you can add the suffix '-ish' to almost any adjective you like? Soonish, coldish, warmish? And you can add it to numbers, too, to say that you will be arriving at the party at, well, sixish.

Far Out, Man!

Another handy little word is 'out'. Spiders can 'creep you out'. You can be 'grossed out' by watching someone pick their nose and eat it. You can even be 'weirded out' if you encounter something very strange. And if you watch a psycho-thriller like *The Shining*, you could be freaked out for weeks.

After a long week at work, when you feel totally 'stressed out', you may end up 'zonking out' on the couch because you

1 **quaintness:** Schrulligkeit. | 3 **wilderness** ['wɪldənɪs]: Wildnis. | 6 **tidbit:** Leckerbissen. | 11 **far out:** super, toll. | 14 **to encounter:** stoßen auf, begegnen.

are so tired you can't drag yourself to bed. In fact, you may decide to stay home on Friday night and 'chill out'.

It can be an internal reaction:

He **spazzed out** (acted spastic, uncoordinated).

She **zonked out** (fell asleep).

They **pooped out** (ran out of energy).

He **spaced out** (was unconcentrated).

She **chilled out** (relaxed).

He **vegged out** (acted like a vegetable/'couch potato').

They **pigged out** (ate too much).

She **freaked out** (went crazy temporarily).

He **wimped out** (gave up like a **namby-pamby**, see p. 26).

He **zoned out** (was in stand-by mode).

Or as a result of something:

It **creeped me out**. (It was creepy. See also **the creeps**, p. 117.)

It **grossed me out**. (It was gross/disgusting.)

It **weirded me out**. (It was weird.)

It **spooked me out**. (It was spooky, scary.)

It **freaked me out**. (It was freaky, unnerving.)

15 **creepy:** unheimlich, gruselig. | 19 **spooky:** gespenstisch. | 20 **freaky:** durchgeknallt, irre.

But watch OUT for 'luck out'. If you win the lottery, you've 'lucked out' in American English. In Britain and Australia it means the opposite: *The team made it to the semi-finals, but unfortunately lucked out (lost) in the final game.*

Common Yiddish Words

A number of Yiddish words have been borrowed into the English language, especially in the U.S. Some of them are originally from Hebrew such as 'chutzpah' (**to have balls**, see p. 68) and to 'schmooze' (to **hob-nob**, see p. 25), but many have a German etymology. Can you guess what these English words mean?

kaput	a putz
schlong	oy vey!
dreck	schmalz
kitsch	schmuck
klutz	schnozz
to nosh	schtick
to schlep	

KAPUT broken; SCHLONG penis; DRECK low quality article; KITSCH junk; KLUTZ a clumsy person; TO NOSH to snack; TO SCHLEP to haul or drag; A PUTZ a jerk (Trottel); OY VEY! oh no (oh weh!); SCHMALZ excessive sentimentality; SCHMUCK jerk; SCHNOZZ nose; SCHTICK a certain behaviour used to get attention

Let's Play Ball

English has borrowed many terms, situations and activities from sports into everyday usage. You might know 'hitting below the belt', or 'throw in the towel' from boxing, or to 'win by a nose' from horse racing. Below are some of the most common idioms from baseball and cricket.

to touch base to make contact and briefly inform someone of your plans. In baseball, players must touch each base as they run by it. *We will touch base before the meeting.*

a whole new ball game a completely new situation. In baseball, this is when the losing team suddenly takes the lead. *After the boss resigned it was a whole new ball game at work.*

to strike out to fail. In baseball, a strike is when the batter swings and misses the ball, or when the batter misjudges the pitch and doesn't swing. After three strikes he has 'struck out' and his turn at bat is over. *The boss told me after I made two serious mistakes: 'One more strike and you're out!'*

grandstanding doing something to get the attention of a large crowd. In baseball, a player who shows off for the fans is 'grandstanding'. *The politicians at the convention spent half their time on stage grandstanding.*

in the ballpark within a limited range. In baseball, the ballpark limits where the game is played. Also used with an estimate: *Can you give me a ballpark estimate how much that house might cost?*

8 **base:** (Baseball) Mal, Standpunkt. | 14 **batter:** Schlagmann/-frau. | 16 **pitch:** (Baseball) Wurf. | 17 **bat:** Baseballschläger, -keule.

It's Just Not Cricket!

to be on a sticky wicket to be in a difficult situation. In cricket, when the wicket area is wet and difficult to play on due to rain, it is referred to as 'sticky'. *'We only have 20 pounds to last us until the end of the month.' – 'Yes, we're on a sticky wicket.'*

to hit somebody for six to be completely shocked. If the cricket ball is hit over the boundary without it touching the ground, the batsman receives six runs (points). *When his wife left him, it really hit him for six.*

a hat-trick three successful events in a row. In the past, when a bowler managed three wickets in a row, he was rewarded with a hat. If you are *on a hat-trick* that means you have managed something twice and are hoping for a third success.

to bowl someone over to be surprised in a good way. In cricket, the bowler must try to knock over the stumps. If he manages to do this, there is a sudden noise and the batsman is out. *I was bowled over by your generous gift.*

It's just not cricket! It's unfair and dishonest. Cricket has a reputation as a gentlemen's game, played by honest and upright people. *You can't copy your essay from the Internet. It's just not cricket!*

to have a good innings to have had a long life. In cricket, if

2 **wicket:** Spielbahn (längliche Fläche inmitten des Spielfeldes, auf der das Hauptgeschehen – der Kampf zwischen Werfer und Schläger – stattfindet). | 8 **boundary:** (Kricket) Spielfeldgrenze. | 9 **batsman:** Schlagmann. | 11 **in a row:** nacheinander. | 12 **bowler:** (Kricket) Werfer. | **wicket:** hier: Ausscheiden eines Schlagmannes. | 24 **innings:** Innings (Spieldurchgang im Kricket, währenddessen eine Mannschaft das Schlagrecht besitzt).

the batsman scores 80, or 90 or even 100 runs in an innings, then he has been very successful. *My grandfather lived to be 96; he had a good innings.*

Colourful Comparisons … Aussie Style

Imagine yourself sitting at the table after an absolutely delicious meal where you have stuffed yourself. You have eaten far too much and feel full to the point of exploding. The hostess asks you if you would like more, but you couldn't take another bite. You *might* respond that you are 'full as a fat lady's sock' or 'as full as a tick' or 'as full as a goog' (Australian for 'egg') or 'as full as the last bus'.

In fact, Australians love making comparisons. Some are quite sarcastic:

as funny as a fart in an elevator

as useful as an ashtray on a motorbike

as useful as tits on a bull

better than a poke in the eye with a burnt stick

But most are quite 'picturesque' because of the image they evoke:

4 **Aussie** (coll.): Australien; Australier(in); australisch. | 6 **to stuff:** vollstopfen. | 10 **tick** (zool.): Zecke. | 14 **fart:** Furz. | 17 **poke:** Stoß. | 19 **to evoke:** hervorrufen, evozieren.

as busy as a one-legged man at an arse-kicking competition

as dry as an Englishman's towel

as dry as a witch's tit (thirsty)

as cold as a polar bear's bum

to be off like a bride's nightie (leave quickly)

to carry on like a pork chop (to get overly excited about something trivial)

to be like a bull in a china shop (clumsy)

to be lower than a snake's armpit

to have more chins than a Chinese phone book

4 **bum** (coll.): Hintern. | 8 **china:** Porzellan. | 9 **armpit:** Achselhöhle.

Let's Get Silly

The motto here is 'the sillier, the better'.

What goes ha-ha-ha plop?
Someone laughing their head off.

Books That Were Never Written

Read these titles out loud!

Miniskirt Fashion by C. Moore Legg

How to Check a Pulse by Izzy Dead

Rusty Bed Springs by I. P. Knightly

Falling Off a Cliff by Eileen Dover

Be Prepared by Justin Case

Why Should I Walk? by Iona Carr

Gotta Go by C. U. Later

The Lost Soul by Werram Eye

Basic Architecture by Bill Ding

Deep in Debt by Owen A. Lott

Long Walk Home by Misty Bus

A Week in the Desert by Anita Bath

A Safe Hitchhiker's Guide by Ren Tacar

My Life as a Dyslexic by Bass Ackwards

Interesting Sexual Positions by Bendo Verr

The Bearded Chinaman by Harry Chin

The Numbers Game by Cal Q. Later

Fear of Success by Willie Douet

5 **bedspring:** Bettfeder. | 16 **dyslexic:** Legastheniker(in).

Smart Phones by Ann Droid

Cat's Revenge by Claude Balls

Sitting on the Beach by Sandy Cheeks

Something Smells by I. Ben Phartin

Oscar Nominations by Holly Wood

Wicked Breath by Hal E. Tosis

Easy Money by Robyn Banks

The Science of Optometry by Seymour Clearly

The Last Supper by M. T. Potts

How to Destroy Buildings by Dinah Mite

Transportation in the Middle Ages by Orson Cart

Answering the Questions of the Universe by Howard I. Know

Quite in the Libary! by Candy Sbel

How to Write a Mystery Novel by Paige Turner

The Great English Breakfast by Chris P. Bacon

Ugly Fingernails by I. Bightem

Meeting in France by Ron D. Voo

A *Trip to the Dentist* by Lord Howard Hurts

2 **Claude Balls:** *clawed balls:* zerkratzte Eier (Hoden). | 3 **cheek:** hier: Pobacke. | 4 **Phartin:** *farting* (*to fart:* furzen). | 6 **wicked:** hier: schlecht. | **Hal E. Tosis**: *halitosis:* Mundgeruch, Halitosis. | 8 **optometry:** Optometrie (Messen und Bewerten der Sehfunktion). | 11 **Orsen Cart:** *(h)orse 'n' cart: Pferdekutsche.* | 15 **Chris P:** *crispy:* knusprig.

So Thirsty by Phillip A. Glass

Boring Meetings by I. M. Yawning

Traditional Chinese Agriculture by Hu Flung Poo

Surveillance Handbook by I. C. Ewe

Memorable Farts by Lett M. Rip

When She Left by Mister Terribly

Hurry Up! by Arnt U. Dunnyet

Big Waves by Sue Nami

Lullaby by Sarah Nade

Where's My Stuff? by I. Ben Robbed

Desert Crossing by Rhoda Kamel

Don't Touch! by Hans Off

The Haunted House by Hugo First

All About Donkeys by Jack Asse

Skunks by P. Hugh

Modern Music by M. P. Three

I Love Chocolate by Emmie Nemms

Starbucks by Megan Coffee

3 **Hu Flung Poo:** *who flung poo?* (*to fling – flung – flung:* schleudern, werfen; *poo* [coll.]: Scheiße). | 4 **surveillance** [sə'veɪləns]: Überwachung. | 5 **memorable:** denkwürdig; unvergesslich. | **Lett M. Rip:** *let (th)em rip* (*to let rip* [coll.]: loslegen; *to rip a fart* [coll.]: einen Furz lassen). | 13 **haunted house:** Spukhaus. | 14 **Jack Asse:** *jackass*: Esel(hengst); Blödmann.

BaaBaa by Fee-Ling Sheepish

German Barbers by Herr Dresser

Race to the Bathroom by Willie Makit, illustrated by Betty Wont

Books that were never written (for a good reason!):

Famous Italian War Heroes

Different Ways to Spell 'Bob'

Detroit – A Travel Guide

Ethiopian Tips on World Dominance

Staple Your Way to Success

The Amish Phone Book

A Nerd's Guide to Fashion

Satisfied Windows Users

Feminists Men Want to Marry

101 Things to Do on a Sunny Day in England

More books that were never written:

Spotted Owl Recipes by the WWF

The Importance of Telling the Truth by Bill Clinton

One Wife is Best by Henry VIII

17 **spotted owl:** Fleckenkauz (als potenziell gefährdet eingestufter Eulenvogel in Nordamerika).

How to Remember Your Lines by Charlie Chaplin

My Life's Memories by Ronald Reagan

Things I Can't Afford by Bill Gates

Kids' Riddles + Jokes

Riddles and jokes are fun because they play with language.

Why did the chicken cross the road?
To get to the other side.

What did one wall say to the other?
'I'll meet you at the corner.'

What did one ocean say to the other ocean?
Nothing, they just waved.

Why do bees hum?
Because they don't know the words!

How do you catch a squirrel?
Climb up a tree, and act like a nut.

Why did the burglar take a bath?
Because he wanted to make a clean getaway.

Why did the girl throw the clock?
She wanted to see time fly.

4 **riddle:** Rätsel. | 14 **squirrel:** Eichhörnchen. | 15 **nut: 1.** Nuss; **2.** Spinner(in), Bekloppte(r). | 17 **to make a clean getaway:** schnell abhauen.

Knock Knock!

Knock knock jokes are especially appreciated by children. They have been around for nearly a century. The trick to a good knock knock joke is that the name of the knocker morphs into a different word in the final line. Try reading these out loud with a partner:

Knock, knock.
Who's there?
Annie.
Annie, who?
Annie one you like!

Knock, knock.
Who's there?
Harry.
Harry who?
Harry up, it's cold out here!

Knock, knock.
Who's there?
Noah.
Noah who?
Noah good place we can get something to eat?

Knock, knock.
Who's there?
Justin.
Justin who?
Justin time for dinner.

4 **to morph into s.th.:** sich in etwas verwandeln.

Knock, knock.
Who's there?
Nana.
Nana who?
Nana your business.

Knock, knock
Who's there?
Ben.
Ben who?
Ben knocking for 10 minutes.

Knock, knock.
Who's there?
Norma Lee.
Norma Lee who?
Norma Lee I don't go around knocking on doors.

Knock, knock!
Who's there?
Kent.
Kent who?
Kent you tell?

Knock, knock!
Who's there?
Sabina.
Sabina who?
Sabina long time since I've seen you!

Doctor, Doctor!

Doctor, doctor, everyone keeps ignoring me.
Next please!

Doctor, doctor, I keep thinking there are two of me.
One at a time please.

Doctor, doctor, I've lost my memory.
When did this happen?
When did what happen?

Doctor, doctor, my son has swallowed my pen, what should I do?
Use a pencil until I get there.

Doctor, doctor, I feel like a pack of cards.
I'll deal with you later.

Doctor, doctor, can I have a second opinion?
Of course, come back tomorrow!

Doctor, doctor, I keep thinking I'm God.
When did this start?
Well first I created the Sun, then the Earth …

Doctor, doctor, I keep thinking I'm invisible.
Who said that?

Doctor, doctor, I feel like a pair of curtains.
Well, pull yourself together.

Doctor, doctor, some days I feel like a teepee and other days I feel like a wigwam.
Hmm, I think you're two tents.

12 **pack of cards:** Kartenspiel. | 19 **invisible:** unsichtbar.

Slightly More Sophisticated …

Bar Jokes

'Bar jokes' always begin with someone walking into a bar …

A horse goes into a bar and walks over to the bartender. The bartender looks at the horse and says: 'Hey buddy, why the long face?'

A man walks into a bar with a slab of asphalt under his arm and says: 'A beer please, and one for the road.'

Two guys walk into a bar. One has a German shepherd and the bouncer stops him: 'No dogs allowed'. The man says, 'It's my seeing eye dog.' The bouncer lets him go by.

His friend also has a dog and decides to try the same thing. The bouncer says, 'Hey buddy, no dogs allowed.' 'He's my seeing eye dog.' 'Nice try, but that's a Chihuahua.' 'A Chihuahua? You mean they gave me a Chihuahua?'

A toothless termite walks into a bar and asks, 'Is the bar tender here?'

Two peanuts walk into a bar. One was assaulted.

A guy with dyslexia walks into a bra.

1 **sophisticated:** niveauvoll, anspruchsvoll. | 4 **bartender:** Barkeeper. | 5 **buddy** (coll.): Kumpel. | 7 **slab (of asphalt):** (Asphalt) Platte. | 8 **one for the road:** (Alkohol) noch einen zum Abgewöhnen. | 9 **German shepherd:** Deutscher Schäferhund. | 10 **bouncer:** Türsteher. | 18 **to be assaulted:** angegriffen werden (Wortspiel mit *salted:* gesalzen). | 19 **dyslexia:** Lese-Rechtschreib-Schwäche, Legasthenie.

What's the Difference between ...?

What's the difference between ignorance and apathy?
I don't know and I don't care.

What's the difference between a sensitive new-age guy and a male chauvinist?
Two beers.

What's the difference between a tyre and 365 condoms?
One is a good year and the other is a great year.

What's the difference between a bird and a fly?
A bird can fly but a fly can't bird.

What's the difference between the government and the Mafia?
One of them is organized.

What's the difference between someone who is trying to lose weight and a virgin?
One is trying to diet and the other is dying to try it.

What's the difference between a man and a pig?
You mean there IS a difference?

Did You Hear the One about the ...

A missionary goes to Africa to visit a very old, primitive tribal community. He talks for half an hour, and then the interpreter stands up and says only four words. Everyone laughs. The missionary is confused. How is this possible? What kind of amazing language is this? Puzzled, he asks the interpreter, 'How did you translate my story, which was so long, into only four

23 **puzzled:** verdutzt, verblüfft.

words?' The interpreter says, 'Story too long, so I say, "He tell joke – laugh!"'

Ship in distress: Mayday! Mayday! We are sinking …
German Coast Guard: What are you sinking about?

Two newlyweds are getting undressed in front of each other for the first time. He takes off his shoes and socks. His toes are all twisted and discoloured.
'What happened to your feet?' his wife asks.
'I had a childhood disease called tolio.'
'Don't you mean polio?'
'No, tolio, it only affects the toes.' He then removes his pants, revealing an awful-looking pair of knees.
'What happened to your knees?' she asked.
'Well, I also had kneesles.'
'Don't you mean measles?'
'No, kneesles – it only affects the knees.'
When he removes his shorts, his wife gasps and says, 'Don't tell me … you also had … smallcox!'

A doctor examines a female patient and then asks her, 'Do you smoke after having sexual intercourse?' She replies 'I don't know, I've never looked.'

Two highway workers are busy working at a construction site when a big car with diplomatic license plates pulls up. 'Parlez-vous français?' the driver asks them. The two workers just stare at him.
'Sprechen Sie Deutsch?' The two continue to stare.

3 **(to be) in distress:** (Schiff) in Seenot (sein). | 5 **newlywed:** Frischvermählte(r). | 17 **to gasp:** tief einatmen; nach Luft schnappen. | 18 **smallcox:** Wortspiel mit *smallpox:* Pocken, Blattern und *small cocks* (vulg.): kleine Pimmel. | 23 **to pull up:** anhalten.

'Fala português?' Neither worker says a word.

'Parlate Italiano?' Still no response.

Finally, the man drives off in disgust.

One worker turns to the other and says, 'Gee, maybe we should learn a foreign language …'

'What for? That guy knew four of them and what good did it do him?'

A man goes to the doctor's with a cucumber up his nose, a carrot in his left ear and a banana in his right ear. 'What's the matter with me?' he asks the doctor.

The doctor replies, 'You're not eating properly.'

Did you hear about the dyslexic, agnostic insomniac?

He stayed up all night wondering if there really was a dog.

And finally …

What did the farmer say when he lost his tractor?

'Where's my tractor?'

3 **in disgust:** angewidert; hier: empört, entrüstet. | 4 **gee:** Mensch! | 12 **dyslexic:** mit Lese-Rechtschreib-Schwäche, legasthenisch. | **insomniac:** an Schlaflosigkeit Leidende(r).

Being Indirect

Sometimes it's better not to say what you think, especially if you're thinking something nasty, rude, or taboo. English has lots of ways to beat around the bush . . .

BOSS. I'm not quite sure how to say this, but I am afraid your current situation has become subject to our continuing workforce adjustment strategy.
EMPLOYEE. You mean I'm fired?
BOSS. You could say that.

4 **to beat around the bush:** um den heißen Brei herumreden. | 7 **workforce:** Arbeitskräfte. | **adjustment strategy:** Anpassungsstrategie.

Euphemisms

Don't miss the game on page 168.

A euphemism replaces a direct and uncomfortable expression with a mild or vague one. Euphemisms make it easier to talk about difficult subjects, such as death and bodily functions. Let's say you have just taken your old, sick pet dog to the vet. Clearly, it's much easier to say 'we had Rover put down' than to say 'the vet killed Rover'. English speakers use euphemisms in many contexts including 'going to the bathroom', 'being in the family way' or 'getting the axe'.

Since death is such a heavy subject, there are many ways to talk about it light-heartedly.

Did you hear about the Italian Chef that died?
He pasta way.

Did she die? Yes, she ...

kicked the bucket

went to meet her maker

is under green blankets

croaked / croaked it (AusE)

fell off the perch

gave up the ghost (also for broken machines)

7 **to put down** (fig.): (Haustier) einschläfern. | 9 f. **to be in the family way:** in anderen Umständen sein. | 10 **to get the axe:** abgesägt (entlassen) werden (*axe:* Axt, Beil). | 19 **to croak (it)** (coll.): abkratzen. | 20 **perch:** (Vogel) Sitzstange; Hochsitz.

went to the big ____________ in the sky
(blank filled in with a place: farm, beach, office etc.)

Is he dead? Yes, he's ...

pushing up daisies

resting in peace

six feet under

wearing a toe tag (ID tag at morgue)

Know a widow? What about her dead husband?

You mean her *late* husband?

Were they killed by the mafia? Yes, they were ...

rubbed out

snuffed out

bumped off

Something (almost) everybody does, but may not admit to ...

spanking the monkey

jerkin' the gherkin

4 **daisy:** Gänseblümchen. | 7 **tag:** Schild(chen). | **morgue:** Leichenschauhaus. | 11 **to rub out:** ausradieren. | 12 **to snuff out:** auslöschen. | 16 **to spank:** verhauen. | 17 **to jerk:** rucken, zucken. | **gherkin:** Gewürzgurke.

beating the bishop

spending time with Madame Palm and her five sisters

And for the ladies ...

doing some circle work in the lower paddock (AusE)

brushing the beaver

petting the pussy cat

squeezing the peach

having a private party

Something (almost) everybody does, and admits to ...

making love

going all the way

hitting a home run

sowing your wild oats

having a taste of forbidden fruit

doing the horizontal hustle

dipping your wick

4 **paddock:** Koppel, Feld. | 5 **beaver:** Biber; hier (vulg.): Muschi. | 7 **peach:** Pfirsich; hier (vulg.): Muschi. | 12 **to hit a home run:** (Baseball) einen Homerun erzielen. Bei einem Homerun gelingt es dem Schlagmann, infolge eines eigenen Schlages alle vier Male abzulaufen und mit Erreichen des Schlagmals einen *Run* zu erzielen. | 13 **wild oat:** Wildhafer. | 15 **hustle:** (Gesellschaftstanz) Hustle, Discofox. | 16 **wick:** Docht; (sl.) Penis.

Expecting?

If a single woman gets 'knocked up', then her father might insist on a 'shotgun wedding' in which the bridegroom has no choice but to do the right thing and marry the girl if he values his life. Ideally, they should get married before anyone notices she 'has a bun in the oven' or is 'up the duff'.

Going to the Toilet

Nobody likes talking about urination and defecation. Some people don't even like to mention the word 'toilet'. Americans prefer to say 'bathroom' or 'restroom'. In America even pets 'go to the bathroom'. They 'do their business' in the litter box or leave their 'pooties' on the lawn.

Most often people refer to the place:

Saying where you are going is often easier than saying what you are going to do when you get there. So, people say they are going to the 'restroom' (AE), the 'loo' (BE), the 'john' or the 'can'[9] (AE), or the 'dunny' (AusE).

... or they refer to doing something else:

When you get to the restroom, of course, you do **not** have a rest. You 'answer the call of nature', 'powder your nose', or 'spend a penny' (BE).

9 The terms 'john' and 'can' are generally only used by men.

2 **to knock up** (coll.): schwängern. | 3 **shotgun wedding:** Mussehe. | 4 **to value:** (wert)schätzen. | 6 **bun:** Brötchen. | **up the duff** (coll.): (ungewollt) schwanger. | 8 **defecation:** Darmentleerung, Stuhlgang. | 11 **litter box:** Katzenklo. | 12 **pooty:** Hundekacke.

When directly talking about the act of urinating, people couch their embarrassment in funny expressions. They 'take a leak' or a 'slash'. In Australia, they 'wet their boots', 'point percy at the porcelain' or 'shake hands with their wife's best friend'. Americans 'worship Urinadio'.

Some come here to sit and think,
Some come here to shit and stink,
But I come here to scratch my balls
And read the bullshit on the walls.

Others may come here to 'take a dump' or 'pinch a loaf'. And if you have to *run* to the bathroom, then you 'have the trots' or 'the runs', or, if you have been travelling, 'Montezuma's revenge'.

Beans, beans, the musical fruit,
The more you eat, the more you toot,
The more you toot, the better you feel,
So eat your beans at every meal!

Most people avoid 'tooting' in public, and references to this bodily function range from the vague to the humorous. To 'pass wind', or to 'break wind' are probably the most polite ways of referring to 'flatulence' (which is what a doctor would call it). Some expressions emphasize the smell ('to cut the cheese') and some the noise ('to step on a frog' or 'to let one rip'). Unannounced flatulence that really stinks is known as

2 **to couch** [kaʊtʃ] (fig.): (in Worte) kleiden, fassen. | 8 **balls** (pl., sl.): Eier (Hoden). | 10 **to pinch (off):** abschnüren. | 11 **the trots** (coll.): Renneritis. | 23 f. **to let one rip** (coll.): einen fahren lassen (*to rip:* [zer]reißen).

'silent but deadly' (SBD) or 'silent but violent'. This endangers unfortunate bystanders in elevators, cars, movie theaters, meeting rooms, and so on.

Another less-than-pleasant bodily function is vomiting. In fact, vomiting is so revolting it makes you want to puke, literally! It is, in fact, contagious. There are some short, evocative verbs to describe this: hurl, barf, spew, heave, ralph, retch, and puke. But to ease the pain (and smell), there are also some funny expressions that describe this unfortunate condition:

talk on the white porcelain telephone

toss your cookies

enjoy yourself in reverse

have a Technicolor yawn

feed the fishes

Job Loss

Although not related to the body, job loss is also a taboo described by numerous indirect euphemisms. 'To be given the sack' or 'to be sacked' dates back to receiving your last sack of coins or being handed your sack of tools to take home. Because job loss is such a serious subject, there are some gentler ways to describe it: 'to be made redundant', 'to be laid off', 'to

5 **revolting:** ekelhaft, abstoßend (von frz. *révolter:* zurück-, umwälzen). | **to puke** (coll.): spucken, kotzen. | 6 **contagious:** ansteckend. | **evocative:** sinnträchtig, atmosphärisch. | 8 **to ease:** lindern. | 11 **to toss:** werfen, schleudern. | 21 **redundant:** überflüssig.

be let go'. More picturesque are: 'to get the axe' or 'to get the boot'.

Companies have their own way of breaking bad news. Don't be fooled if your boss suggests a 'career change opportunity' or an 'outplacement' for you. This is not a promotion. Beware of:

coerced transition

derecruitment

dehiring

destaffing

downsizing

negotiated departure

workforce adjustment

That sucked!

A failed presentation may be called 'less than impressive', 'underwhelming', or a 'lame performance', if it got a 'tepid' reaction from the audience. Whether it 'went over like a lead balloon' or was a complete disaster is debatable. But what you can say is that your explanations were 'as clear as mud'.

3 **to break bad news**: schlechte Nachrichten überbringen. | 3 f. **don't be fooled:** lass dich / lassen Sie sich nicht täuschen. | 5 **beware of ...:** Vorsicht vor ...! | 6 **coerced:** erzwungen. | **transition:** Wechsel, Übergang. | 12 **workforce:** Arbeitskräfte; Belegschaft. | **adjustment:** Anpassung. | 13 **that sucks** (AE, coll.): das ist Scheiße! | 15 **tepid** (fig.): lauwarm. | 16 f. **to go over/down like a lead** [led] **balloon:** überhaupt nicht ankommen (*lead:* Blei).

Being Drunk

Whether the police describe your condition as 'under the influence' or you feel you've had 'a drop too much', there are lots of slang words to describe being drunk. You can be 'boozed up', 'tipsy', 'tiddly', 'squiffy', 'tight', 'half-cut', 'Brahms and Liszt', 'well-oiled', 'pickled', 'bottled', or 'tired and emotional'. You can be as 'drunk as a lord' or as 'drunk as a skunk', or as 'pissed as a newt' (BE).

Here is a historical overview of being drunk. Many of these are still in use – they are marked in **bold**.

1900s	**blotto** (AusE), ginned, pie-eyed, pifflicated, rosey, saturated, shellacked, **tanked**
1910s /20s	**crocked** (AE), fried, hooted, juiced, **lubricated**, **paralytic**, **pissed** (BE, AusE), **plastered**, polluted
1930s /40s	**bombed** (AE), flooey, looped, rum-dumb, **shit-faced**, swacked
1950s /60s	bevvied, boxed, crashed, **sloshed**, **smashed**, **wrecked**, zonked
1970s /80s	**legless** (AusE), **loaded** (AE)
1990s/2000s	bladdered, blootered, lagered, rat-arsed, ratted, **wankered** (BE)

2 f. **under the influence** (coll.): betrunken. | 4 **boozed up** (coll.): besoffen (*booze:* Fusel, Alk). | 5 **tipsy:** beschwipst. | **tiddly** (coll.): beschwipst. | **squiffy** (coll.): angesäuselt. | **tight** (coll.): voll, blau. | **half-cut** (coll.): besoffen. | 5 f. **Brahms and Liszt:** Rhyming Slang für *pissed* (vulg.): besoffen. | 8 **newt:** Wassermolch. | 10 **in bold:** fettgedruckt.

Drunkeness can lead to idiotic behaviour. English has lots of words for idiots. Someone whose 'elevator doesn't go to the top floor' can be called a moron, an imbecile, a jerk, a dolt, a retard, a buffoon, a git, an ignoramus, a nitwit, a pea-brain, a birdbrain, an airhead, a dope, a **nincompoop** (see p. 16), a cretin, a numskull, a schmuck, a twerp, or simply a dummy.

More picturesquely speaking, an idiot is ...

not the sharpest tool in the shed

not the sharpest knife in the drawer

not firing on all cylinders

two sandwiches short of a picnic

one card short of a full deck

one brick short of a load

knitting with one needle

driving with only three wheels

a few beers short of a six pack

a few dice short of Yahtzee

as thick as two short planks

3 **imbecile** ['ɪmbɪsiːl]: Schwachkopf. | 4 **ignoramus** [ˌɪgnə'reɪməs]: Nichtswisser(in), Ignorant(in). | 11 **short of:** weniger als. | 12 **deck (of cards):** Kartenspiel. | 14 **to knit** [nɪt]: stricken. | 17 **Yahtzee:** (Würfelspiel) Yahtzee, Kniffel.

And if someone is absent-minded, you could say they are ...

out to lunch

a space cadet

a basket case

Are you mad?

Beyond being a basket case is 'mad'. But there are two meanings of 'mad'. When someone is crazy or 'off their rocker', you can say they have 'a screw loose' or they have 'lost their marbles'. If something gives them the 'screaming irrits' (AusE), then they are mad in the sense of angry, and they can be described as 'going berserk' or 'going ballistic'.

If you are disorganized or forgetful, people might say that you ...

are a day late and a dollar short

would be late for your own funeral

couldn't find your way out of a paper bag

couldn't organize a piss-up in a brewery

have a mind like a sieve

1 **absent-minded:** geistesabwesend. | 8 **rocker:** (Roll-)Kufe; Schaukelstuhl. | 9 f. **marble:** Murmel. | 18 **brewery:** Brauerei.

Be Careful What You Say

In order to be as polite as possible, we now have politically correct speech. It helps us describe characteristics without offending anyone.

(bald) differently hirsute

(big nose) nasally gifted

(blind) visually challenged

(computer illiterate) technologically challenged

(crippled) differently abled, physically challenged

(deaf) hearing impaired

(dwarf, midget) vertically challenged

(fat) weight challenged

(geek, nerd) socially challenged

(messy) differently organized

(retarded) mentally challenged, people with learning difficulties

(stupid) intellectually challenged

(sickly) failing to fulfil their wellness potential

(white trash) Caucasian culturally-disadvantaged

3 f. **to offend:** kränken. | 5 **hirsute** ['hɜːsjuːt]: stark behaart. | 8 **illiterate** [ɪ'lɪtərɪt]: ungebildet, unwissend. | 11 **dwarf:** Zwerg(in). | **midget:** Kleinwüchsige(r). | 13 **geek:** Außenseiter(in); Freak. | 15 **retarded:** zurückgeblieben. | 19 **white trash** (AE, pej.): weißes Pack. | **Caucasian:** Weiße(r).

Politically correct terms are now also used for jobs, positions, and situations that are perceived as less desirable:

(bum) homeless person

(garbage man) sanitation engineer

(housewife) domestic engineer

(prostitute) escort

(retiree) senior citizen

Initially, political correctness was introduced to rid the language of 'loaded' expressions to avoid being negative. However, PC has been taken to extremes, especially by young people, as can be seen in the following PC descriptions of students:

These days, students aren't **lazy**, they're …
motivationally deficient.

They're not **late**, they just have a …
rescheduled arrival time.

They don't have **bad hair days**, they suffer from …
rebellious follicle syndrome.

They don't have **smelly sport socks**, they have …
odour-retentive athletic footwear.

2 **to perceive:** wahrnehmen, erkennen. | **desirable:** erstrebenswert. | 3 **bum** (coll.): Penner(in). | 4 **sanitation:** Abfallentsorgung. | 7 **retiree:** Ruheständler(in). | 16 **to reschedule:** umplanen, neu terminieren. | 20 **odour-retentive:** den Duft aufnehmend/bewahrend.

They're not **shy**. They're …
conversationally selective.

They don't **talk a lot**. They're just …
abundantly verbal.

And it's not called **gossip** any more. It's …
the speedy transmission of near-factual information.

What's on TV is not the **worst** show. It's the …
least best.

How to say something is **obvious**:
Is the Pope Catholic?
Does the bear shit in the woods?

How to say something is **futile**:
It's like rearranging deck chairs on the Titanic.
It's like nailing jelly to the ceiling.

How to say something makes you feel **uncomfortable**: When something makes you feel anxious, nervous, uneasy or scared, it gives you …

the willies,

the shivers,

the jitters,

the creeps,

the heebie-jeebies (see p. 25),

the goosebumps.

4 **abundantly:** reichlich, im Übermaß. | 12 **futile:** sinnlos.

Word Play

Words can be the source of hours of fun . . .

Rearrange the letters below to spell part of the human body that is more useful when erect.

P N E S I

Spine, of course (Wirbelsäule)

4 **erect:** aufrecht, aufgerichtet; steif, erigiert.

Anagrams

An anagram is a word created by rearranging the letters of another word. Sometimes this is easy (god/dog, see p. 102), but the more creative, the better. Ideally, the anagram refers in some way to the original word:

airfields	*aid fliers*
the aristocracy	*a rich Tory caste*
athletics	*lithe acts*
the countryside	*no city dust here*
earnestness	*a stern sense*
the eyes	*they see*
the holy gospel	*helps theology*
postponed	*Stopped? No.*
a sentence of death	*faces one at the end*
a shoplifter	*has to pilfer*
Southern California	*hot sun or life in a car*
Western Union	*no wire unsent*
astronomers	*moon starers*
Ivanhoe by Sir Walter Scott	*a novel by a Scottish writer*
Ronald Wilson Reagan	*Insane Anglo Warlord*

6 **airfield:** Flugplatz. | 8 **lithe:** geschmeidig, gelenkig. | 10 **stern:** ernst. | 14 **to face s.o.:** jdm. gegenüberstehen. | 15 **to pilfer:** klauen. | 17 **wire:** Telegramm.

Salman Rushdie	*Dare shun Islam!*
Clint Eastwood	*Old West Action*

Spoonerisms

William Archibald Spooner (1844–1930) was an Englishman who taught at Oxford. He is remembered today for his 'bird-watching', or rather 'word-botching'. Everybody makes mistakes like this sometimes, but Spooner was famous for it. In most cases, the switch involves the initial consonants:

'peas and carrots' → 'keys and parrots'

'bad salad' → 'sad ballad'

'master plan' → 'plaster man'

'heating and plumbing' → 'pleating and humming'

'Washington's Birthday' → 'Birthington's Washday'

'Tale of Two Cities' → 'Sale of Two Titties'

'block of flats' → 'flock of bats'

However, sometimes people switch entire words:

We must get to the problem of the bottom.

I wouldn't send a knight out on a dog like this.

1 **to shun:** meiden, sich fernhalten von. | 6 **word-botching:** Wortstümperei. | 8 **switch:** Tausch, Wechsel. | 9 **parrot:** Papagei. | 12 **pleating:** Fälteln, Plissieren. | **humming:** Summen. | 14 **titty:** Titte. | 15 **flock of bats:** Fledermausschwarm. | 18 **knight:** Ritter.

I can remember your name, I just can't think of your face.

A waist is a terrible thing to mind.

Spoonerisms become more common when people are drunk:

I'm not as think as you drunk I am.

Good evening ossifer. I am not under the affluence of incohol.

I don't drink as much as thinkle peep I do.

If you, like Dr. Spooner, are someone who produces a lot of these and if you are planning to rob a bank, then make sure you practise what you are going to say when you storm into the bank with your mask and your gun, otherwise you might end up saying something like this:

Air in the hands mother stickers this is a fuck up!

That's a Pun, Son ...

Puns are a type of word play that combines double meanings and sometimes similar sounding words. They are funniest when they come out spontaneously in conversation. But you can enjoy them even out of context. Sometimes they are a bit tricky because listeners must know various word meanings or the cultural background in order to understand what

5 **affluence:** Reichtum, Überfluss. | 13 **fuck up** (vulg.): Stümperei; Stümper(in).

makes them funny. Here are a few that might tickle your funny bone …

The best way to communicate with fish is to drop them a line.

I couldn't quite remember how to throw a boomerang, but then it came back to me.

He bought a donkey because he thought he might get a kick out of it.

A horse is a stable animal.

I wondered why the baseball was getting bigger and then it hit me.

I used to have a fear of hurdles, but I got over it.

I'm reading a book about anti-gravity. It's impossible to put down.

It's not that the man did not know how to juggle, he just didn't have the balls to do it.

When William joined the army he disliked the phrase 'fire at will'.

A hole has been found in the nudist camp wall. The police are looking into it.

1 f. **to tickle s.o.'s funny bone:** jdn. amüsieren. | 3 **to drop a line: 1.** eine (Angel-)Leine auswerfen; **2.** ein paar Zeilen schreiben. | 5 **to come back to s.o.** (fig.): jdm. wieder einfallen. | 6 f. **to get a kick out of s.th.:** (Idiom) großen Spaß an etwas haben. | 8 **stable:** (Adj.) stabil, beständig; (Nomen) Stall. | 10 **to hit s.o.** (fig.): jdm. aufgehen/auffallen. | 11 **hurdle:** Hürde. | 12 f. **to put down:** (Buch) aus der Hand legen. | 14 **to juggle:** jonglieren. | 15 **to have the balls** (coll.): den Nerv/Mut haben. | 16 f. **fire at will:** Feuer frei! | 19 **to look into** (fig.): (Polizei) ermitteln.

No one knew she had a dental implant until it came out in a conversation.

The butcher backed up into the meat grinder and got a little behind in his work.

You want to clone yourself? Now wouldn't that be just like you!

Sleeping comes so naturally to me, I can do it with my eyes closed.

I've been to the dentist several times so I know the drill.

For a while, Houdini used a lot of trap doors in his act, but he was just going through a stage.

When the grape got stepped on, it let out a little whine.

"Can you give me the ... ahh, ummm, the ...?"

When you have a word on the tip of your tongue, you can either struggle to remember it, mumble 'mmm', 'ah', or you can use one of the many useful words that English has for this purpose: 'thingy', 'thingamajig', 'thingamibob', 'whatchacallit' or 'whatchamacallit'. There's even a plural form: whatchamacallem. Or how about 'diddleebob', or 'doohickey'? Or you can

3 **meat grinder:** Fleischwolf. | 3 f. **to get behind: 1.** in Rückstand kommen; **2.** *behind:* Hintern. | 5 f. **that's just like you** (fig.): das sieht dir ähnlich! | 7 f. **I can do it with my eyes closed** (fig.): Das mache ich mit dem kleinen Finger. | 9 **I know the drill** (fig.): Ich weiß, wie's läuft. | 10 **trap door:** Falltür. | 11 **stage: 1.** Stadium; **2.** Bühne (Houdini war ein berühmter Entfesselungs- und Zauberkünstler). | 12 **grape:** (Wein-)Traube. | **whine:** Jammern, Heulen. | 15 **to mumble:** murmeln, nuscheln.

ask for the 'whatsit', or pens and paper and 'whatnot'. If you can't remember someone's name, you can always say 'what's her face' / 'what's her name' or 'what's his face' / 'what's his name' to refer to them.

Playful Punctuation

Do you realize just how important punctuation is?

If you think hyphens don't matter, then 'you've got another thing coming'. Think about this little misunderstanding:

> The husband lovingly texts that he wants some
> 'extra marital sex',
> and his wife, shocked and hurt, demands:
> 'extra-marital sex? Who is she?'

Where does the colon go in the following?

> We had one problem only Bob knew we weren't wearing underpants.
> - **We had one problem:** only Bob knew we weren't wearing underpants.
> - **We had one problem only:** Bob knew we weren't wearing underpants.
> - **We had one problem only Bob knew:** we weren't wearing underpants.

5 **playful:** spielerisch, scherzhaft. | 7 f. **you've got another thing coming:** da bist du auf dem Holzweg. | 10 **marital:** ehelich.

Consider this:

A woman without her man is nothing.
A woman: without her, man is nothing.

Persuasive Punctuation

Dear Mr. President,

I would like to compliment you. I can't stop thinking that you are one of the best Presidents we have had. So many leaders go ahead and propose policies and then botch the job. We

8 **to botch** (coll.): verpfuschen, vermasseln.

expect it. From you, in years to come, I know we will get better results.

Sincerely,
A Voter

Dear Mr. President,

I would like to compliment you. I can't. Stop thinking that you are one of the best Presidents. We have had so many leaders. Go ahead and propose policies and then botch the job. We expect it from you. In years to come, I know we will get better results.

Sincerely,
A Voter

The Importance of the Oxford Comma

You may have been taught not to put a comma before the word 'and' as in the following:

I speak German, French, English and Greek.

But take a look at this sentence:

I would like to thank my parents, Jane and God.

Are Jane and God her parents? Or is she thanking her parents as well as Jane and God? Just exactly who is she thanking? The sentence should actually read:

I would like to thank my parents, Jane, and God.

This is why many people insist that the 'Oxford comma' is a

good idea.[10] Perhaps the following depiction of the Oxford comma will make the difference clearer.[11]

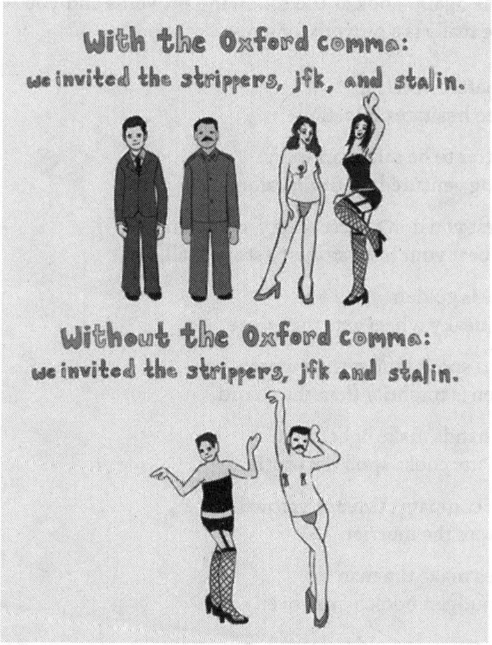

10 It is called the 'Oxford comma' because it is used by the editors at Oxford University Press, but it is also called the 'serial comma'.
11 http://www.thegloss.com/2011/09/19/beauty/why-the-oxford-comma-is-something-you-should-care-about-392/

1 **depiction:** Darstellung.

A Proverb for Every Occasion ...

... or maybe not. If you think proverbs contain great wisdom, then think again. Look at the following proverbs and you will see: there really is a proverb for every occasion.

Look before you leap.
He who hesitates is lost.

It's better to be safe than sorry.
Nothing ventured, nothing gained.

If at first you don't succeed, try, try again.
Don't beat your head against a stone wall.

Silence is golden.
The squeaky wheel gets the grease.

Actions speak louder than words.
The pen is mightier than the sword.

Many hands make light work.
Too many cooks spoil the broth.

Two is company, three is a crowd.
The more the merrier.

Clothes make the man.
Don't judge a book by its cover.

You're never too old to learn.
You can't teach an old dog new tricks.

2 **wisdom:** Weisheit. | 5 **to leap:** springen (*leap – leapt – leapt*). | 8 **to venture:** wagen, riskieren. | **to gain:** gewinnen. | 14 **sword** [sɔːd]: Schwert. | 16 **broth:** Brühe. | 18 **merry:** fröhlich, vergnügt.

Absence makes the heart grow fonder.
Out of sight, out of mind.

Good things come in small packages.
The bigger, the better.

Great minds think alike.
Fools never differ.

When in Rome, do as the Romans do.
To thine own self be true.

8 **thine** (arch.): *your; yours.* | **true:** hier: treu.

A Poem[12]

Ode to My Goldfish

O
Wet
Pet!
Gyles Brandreth (*1948)

12 This is possibly the shortest poem in world history. The author is also known for tossing the world's tiniest pancake (1 mm in diameter).

The English Language

Writing well, improving the English language, saying next to nothing with important-sounding words.

This is the sort of tedious nonsense up with which I will not put.[13]

13 This is often attributed to Winston Churchill, but almost certainly not by him.

4 **tedious** ['tiːdiəs]: langweilig, öde.

Rules for Writers

Written communication is more important than ever – and at the same time it is becoming more and more difficult to get reliable information on how to write well. We have summarized the most important writing rules:

Punctuation

- Avoid un-necessary hyphens.
- Don't use commas, which aren't necessary.
- Avoid excessive use of exclamation marks!!!!!
- Use a full stop it makes your writing easier to read.
- Its important to use apostrophe's in the right places.
- In letters reports summaries e-mails and other texts use commas to separate items in a series.

Spelling

- Remember t he/ importance of being accurit; nea t, and carrful.
- Proofread carefully to see if you any words out.
- Do a spell Czech with a good spell chequer. It wood be careless knot two. If you are old-fashioned, use a dictionery to check your speling.

17 **to proofread:** Korrektur lesen.

Grammar

- Verbs has to agree with their subjects.
- Each pronoun should agree with their antecedent.
- You should never use the second person.
- The passive voice should never be used.
- When a preposition is connected to an adjective, or a pronoun refers back to its antecedent, make sure they stay as close as possible, especially in long sentences that have ten or more words, for the purpose of better readability, to them.
- Hanging from a sentence, one should always avoid leaving a participle.
- No double negatives aren't unnecessary.
- Do not verbify nouns.
- Do not use a preposition to end a sentence with.
- And never start a sentence with a conjunction.
- Make certain all sentences are full and complete. If possible.

Style

- Do not use a big word where a diminutive expression would suffice.
- Conversational expressions in writing are no-nos.
- Avoid the employment of unnecessary excess, additional, extra, superfluous words.
- A writer must be sure to avoid using sexist pronouns in his writing.

3 **antecedent** [ˌæntɪ'siːdənt]: Bezugswort. | 18 **diminutive:** verkleinernd. | 19 **to suffice** [sə'faɪs] (form.): ausreichen, genügen. | 21 **employment:** hier: Verwendung. | **excess:** Übermaß, Überfluss. | 22 **superfluous** [suː'pɜːflʊəs]: überflüssig, verschwenderisch.

- At all costs, avoid clichés as you would the plague.
- Don't approximate. Always be more or less precise.
- Sedulously eschew obfuscatory hyperverbosity or prolixity.
- Avoid pointless repetition, and don't repeat yourself unnecessarily.
- In all written expression, it is paramount, notwithstanding other extraneous considerations, whether they be binding or not, and quite independently of their origin, about which we can sometimes only speculate, to be brief and clear.
- Avoid run-on sentences that just go on, and on, and just keep rambling, and the reader becomes impatient, wishing that the writer would get to the point, but it seems as if the sentence will never stop, so that eventually the reader loses patience and just gives up …
- Never go off on tangents, which are lines that intersect a curve at only one point and were discovered by Euclid, who lived in the sixth century, which was an era dominated by the Goths, who lived in what we now know as Poland.
- It seems to be the case that an author, when he or she is writing, should definitely not make a habit of being unnecessarily wordy or redundant by using too many words that he or she does not really need or require in order to get his or her message across to readers who might find it otherwise incomprehensible.

1 **the plague:** die Pest. | 3 **sedulously:** unermüdlich. | **to eschew** [ɪs'tʃuː]: (ver)meiden. | **obfuscatory:** verwirrend. | **hyperverbosity:** übertriebene Wortfülle; übertriebenes Geschwafel. | **prolixity:** Weitschweifigkeit. | 4 **pointless:** sinnlos. | 6 **to be paramount:** vorrangig sein, Priorität haben. | **notwithstanding:** ungeachtet. | 7 **extraneous:** äußere(r, s). | 11 **to ramble (on):** schwafeln. | 15 **to go off on a tangent:** vom Thema abkommen. | 21 **redundant:** weitschweifig. | 24 **incomprehensible:** unverständlich, unbegreiflich.

Conjugating Very Irregular Verbs[14]

I	am firm
you	are obstinate
he	is a pig-headed fool
we	are Christians
you	are true believers
they	are fanatic fundamentalists
I	daydream
you	are an escapist
she	ought to see a psychiatrist
we	are connoisseurs of fine wines
you	enjoy a drink
they	are alcoholics
I	am voluptuous
you	are plump
she	is obese

14 Two of these 'conjugations' were coined by the British philosopher Bertrand Russell.

3 **obstinate:** starrköpfig, stur. | 4 **pig-headed:** stur, verbohrt. | 11 **connoisseur** [ˌkɒnəˈsɜː]: Kenner. | 14 **voluptuous:** (Figur) üppig. | 15 **plump:** pummelig, mollig. | 16 **obese** [əʊˈbiːs]: fett.

Ghoti and Chips?

If you ask for 'ghoti' you will only get something to eat if you pronounce it right. Here is a hint: look at the spelling of words like 'enou**gh**', 'w**o**men', and 'mo**ti**on'.[15]

And what would you like with your ghoti?

The traditional accompaniment to ghoti are chips. These are made from *ghoughbteighpteaus*. Another hint: look at 'hic-cou**gh**', 'th**ough**', 'de**bt**', '**neigh**bour', '**pt**erodactyl', 'bur**eau**'.[16]

15 The word is, of course, 'fish'. This spelling is often said to have been created by George Bernard Shaw, though nobody has been able to find it in his writings. The story appeared quite suddenly in various publications around 1937, and was soon attached to Shaw's name. But Matt Gordon of the University of Missouri-Columbia found it in an 1874 issue of St James Magazine, which quotes a letter dated 11 December 1855 from the publisher Charles Ollier to Leigh Hunt. Shaw was born in 1856, so he had nothing to do with 'ghoti'. The letter reads: "My son William has hit upon a new method of spelling Fish. As thus: - G.h.o.t.i., Ghoti, fish. Nonsense! say you. By no means, say I. It is perfectly vindicable orthography. You give it up? Well then, here is the proof. Gh is f, as in tough, rough, enough; o is i as in women; and ti is sh, as in mention, attention, &c. So that ghoti is fish." The authors would like to thank Harald Beck for this information.

16 Fish and chips! Chips are made from 'potatoes'.

3 **hint:** Hinweis, Tipp. | 7 f. **hiccough** ['hɪkʌp]: *hiccup:* Schluckauf. | 8 **pterodactyl** [ˌterə'dæktɪl]: Pterodactylus, Flugfinger (Gattung kleiner Kurzschwanzflugsaurier). | **bureau** ['bjʊərəʊ]: Büro; (Möbel) Sekretär.

I Am So Gruntled!

Generally, you won't hear people saying they are 'gruntled' or that something is 'wieldy', but 'disgruntled' ('unsatisfied') and 'unwieldy' ('large and difficult to manage') exist. So 'gruntled' would mean 'happy' or 'satisfied', and 'wieldy' would mean 'easy to manage'. Your skin can be immaculate (if it is pure and has no spots) but we don't call it 'maculate' if it's spotty. Over the years the positive forms have dropped out of the language (or they never existed in the first place). Can you spot the unusual vocabulary in these texts?

YOUNG MAN, 32, sufferable and couth, with a gainly and gentlemanly gait, is looking for his dream girl, who has shevelled hair, and beautifully kempt clothing. Please reply! I would be gruntled to meet you![17]

DEAR YOUNG MAN, I am very mayed that you have not yet found a partner. I am an illusioned young woman. (I haven't met many men with much ruth, but you sound very toward.) I'd like to meet you – it could be very ruptive. I would be appointed to hear from you.[18]

17 The young man is not *insufferable* (unerträglich) and not *uncouth* (ungehobelt). His gait (Gang) is not *ungainly* (ungelenk). His dream girl does not have *dishevelled* (zerzaust) hair, and her clothing is not *unkempt* (ungepflegt). He would not be *disgruntled* (verstimmt) to hear from her.

18 She is not *dismayed* (bestürzt), nor *disillusioned*. She has not met many *ruthless* (rücksichtslos) men, and she thinks he is not *untoward* (unpassend). A meeting would not be *disruptive* (störend) in her life, and she would not be *disappointed* if he contacted her.

English Is a Crazy Language

Let's face it: English is a crazy language.
There is no egg in eggplant, nor ham in hamburger;
neither apple nor pine in pineapple.
And while no one knows what is in a hotdog,
you can be pretty sure it isn't canine.

English muffins were not invented in England,
nor French fries in France.
Sweetmeats are candies, while sweetbreads,
which aren't sweet, are meat.

We take English for granted.
But if we explore its paradoxes,
we find that quicksand can work slowly,
boxing rings are square,
and a guinea pig is neither from Guinea nor is it a pig.
And why is it that writers write,
but fingers don't fing, grocers don't groce,
and hammers don't ham?

If the plural of tooth is teeth,
why isn't the plural of booth beeth?
One goose, two geese. So, one moose, two meese?
Is cheese the plural of choose?
One mouse, two mice.
One louse, two lice.
One house, two hice?

2 **let's face it:** seien wir ehrlich. | 3 **eggplant:** Aubergine. | 6 **canine** ['keɪnaɪn]: Hund. | 8 **French fries** (pl.): Pommes frites. | 11 **to take s.th. for granted:** etwas für selbstverständlich halten. | 13 **quicksand:** Treibsand. | 15 **guinea** ['gɪni] **pig:** Meerschweinchen.

If teachers taught, why didn't preachers praught?
If a vegetarian eats vegetables,
what does a humanitarian eat?

Why do people recite at a play, and play at a recital?
Ship by truck or car and send cargo by ship?
Have noses that run and feet that smell?
Park on driveways and drive on parkways?

How can a slim chance and a fat chance be the same,
while a wise man and a wise guy are opposites?
How can the weather be hot as Hell one day
and cold as Hell another?

When a house burns up, it burns down.
You fill in a form by filling it out
and an alarm clock goes off by going on.

You get in and out of a car,
yet you get on and off a bus.

When the stars are out, they are visible,
but when the lights are out, they are invisible.
And why, when I wind up my watch, I start it,
but when I wind up this essay, I end it?
English is a silly language …
it doesn't know if it is coming or going!

Richard Lederer

3 **humanitarian:** Menschenfreund. | 4 **recital:** (Musik-, Gedicht-)Vortrag; Konzert. | 7 **parkway** (AE): Autobahn. | 9 **wise guy:** Besserwisser. | 17 **visible:** sichtbar.

X Marks the Spot

Why do we need the letter X? We already have other ways of spelling the sound it usually makes. Just think of words like 'locks', 'ticks', 'accident'. They all have an X sound in them. But for some reason, X is loved by advertisers. They use it to attract attention by misspelling words: they write 'sox' instead of 'socks', 'pix' instead of 'pics' or 'pictures', 'jox' instead of 'jocks', 'X-tra' instead of extra, and so on. Maybe 'sex' is the reason X is just so, well, so sexy.

In Australia, XXXX is a brand of beer (pronounced 'four X'), not to be confused with the Mexican beer XX ('Dos Equis', which means 'two Xs' in Spanish). X is also used to make a choice on a form; or mark a location on a map: 'X marks the spot', and it is used as a mathematical symbol for multiplication ($3 \times 4 = 12$) or for an unknown in algebra ($3x = 12$).

If you want to send somebody kisses, you can put Xs at the end of a letter: 'yours forever, xxx'. Historically, Christians signed letters 'yours in Xto' (yours in Christo). People even used to write Xstened and Xstopher, for christened and Christopher. And we all know what Xmas is.[19]

But 'x' isn't all kisses and Xstianity; it also has a dark side. It means 'wrong' on a test. And you can also use X to write something you really shouldn't write: xxxx! In other words, words like xxxx can be Xed out. And it may refer to adult material. An X-rated film is quite naughty, a XXX-rated film, very. X can also refer to a lover – the mysterious Mr X.

19 This has nothing to do with the Christian symbol of the cross, but goes back to the Greek letter at the beginning of *Khristos*.

7 **jock** (coll.): Unterhose. | 25 **X-rated:** nicht jugendfrei (*to rate:* bewerten). | **naughty:** unanständig.

So, is X actually the most useful letter in the alphabet? Possibly. It is the only letter that can be used as a signature on a legal document. But there are other useful letters, too.

Your GPS system will tell you how to get from A to B. Minding your Ps and Qs means behaving yourself, which should be as simple as ABC. And when you leave school you should know the three Rs: Reading, (W)riting, and 'Rithmetic. Lovers of oysters may not know the three Rs, but they will be familiar with the 'R months' (from SeptembeR to ApRil) when they can safely eat shellfish. However, chocolate lovers can enjoy M&Ms all year round.

OK? A-OK! (which just means 'great'). To OD on something means to overdose. (Think of all the rock stars who OD'ed). You can OD on practically anything including watching TV, SMSing, even on drinking OJ (orange juice). If you OD on drugs, you might need an OP in the OR (operation, operating room).

A T-shirt is something you wear. TNT is dynamite! If you order a T-bone steak, you might be lucky and it will be cooked to a T (just right).

In book titles, 'an A to Z' is a comprehensive work ('An A to Z of the Animal Kingdom'). And if you know the Bible from A to Z, then you know it from front to back.

And if you are tired of all this, then you can always catch some Zs as you doze off to sleep. Zzzzzz …

8 **oyster:** Auster. | 10 **shellfish:** Meeresfrüchte. | 21 **comprehensive:** vollständig, umfassend.

Proposals for English Language Reform

A Plan for the *Improvement* of English Spelling[20]

Any reform in spelling should take place over time in order to prevent confusion. In Year 1 that useless letter C would be dropped to be replased either by K or S, and likewise X would no longer be part of the alphabet. The only kase in which C would be retained would be the CH formation, which will be dealt with later.

Year 2 might reform W spelling, so that 'which' and 'one' would take the same konsonant, wile year 3 might well abolish Y replasing it with I. Iear 4 might fiks the G/J anomali wonse and for all. Jenerally, then, the improvement would kontinue iear bai iear.

Iear 5 wud du awai with useless double konsonants, and iears 6–12 or so modifaiing vowlz and the rimeining voist and unvoist konsonants. Bai iear 15 or sou, it wud fainali bi posibl tu meik ius ov thi ridandant letez C, Y and X – bai now jast a memori in the maindz ov ould pipl – tu riplais CH, SH, and TH rispektivli.

Fainali, xen, aafte sam 20 iers ov orxogrefkl riform, wi wud hev a lojikl, kohirnt speling in ius xrewawt xe Ingliy-spiking werld.

20 This text is almost always – in books and on the Internet – attributed to Mark Twain. However, Twain was in favour of spelling reform, something this text obviously ridicules. It is in fact a letter to the editor of the London *Economist* written by M. J. Shields from Durham, who signs his name using his own system: Iors feixfuli, M. J. Xilz. *Economist* [London, England] 16 Jan. 1971.

7 **to retain:** beibehalten.

Another attempt ...

As the previous language reform was not widely accepted, the European Commission has just announced a new agreement. English will now be the official language of the EU rather than German, which was the other possibility. As part of the negotiations, Her Majesty's Government agreed that English spelling can indeed be improved and has accepted a five-year plan to introduce something that will be known as 'Euro-English':

First Year

S will replace the soft C. Sertainly, this will make the sivil servants jump with joy. The hard C will be dropped in favor of the K. This should klear up konfusion and keyboards kan have one less letter.

Sekond Year

There will be growing publik enthusiasm in the sekond year, when the troublesome PH will be replased with the F. This will make words like 'fotograf' 20 % shorter.

Third Year

Publik akseptanse of the new spelling kan be expekted to reach the stage where more komplikated changes are possible. Governments will enkorage the removal of double letters, which have always ben a deterent to akurate speling. Also, al wil agre that the horible mes of the silent E's in the language is disgrasful, and they should be dropt.

Forth Year

Peopl wil be reseptiv to steps such as replasing TH with Z

23 **deterrent:** hier: Hindernis. | 25 **disgraceful:** erbärmlich; skandalös.

and W with V. Ze unesesary O kan be dropt from vords kontaining OU and similar changes vud of kors be aplid to ozer kombinations of leters.

Fifz Yer

After zis fifz yer, ve vil hav a reli sensibl riten styl. Zer vil be no mor trubls or difikultis and evrivun vil find it ezi tu understand ech ozer.

ZE DREM VIL FINALI KUM TRU!

Making Simple Things Complicated

Management making employees jump through (language) hoops:

ENQUIRY. How many feet do mice have?
REPLY. Mice have four feet.
MANAGEMENT. More detail please!

REVISION 1. Mice have five appendages, and four of them are feet.
MANAGEMENT. Why is there no discussion of the fifth appendage!

REVISION 2. Mice have five appendages; four of them are feet and one is a tail.
MANAGEMENT. Feet with no legs? Please explain!

10 f. **to make s.o. jump through hoops:** jdn. nach seiner Pfeife tanzen lassen. | 12 **enquiry:** Nachfrage. | 15 **appendage:** Gliedmaß.

REVISION 3. Mice have four legs, four feet and one tail per unit-mouse.
MANAGEMENT. Confusing! Is that a total of 9 appendages?

REVISION 4. Mice have four leg-foot structures and one tail structure per body.
MANAGEMENT. Does not fully discuss the issue!

REVISION 5. Each mouse comes equipped with four legs and a tail. Each leg is equipped with a foot at the end opposite the body; the tail is not equipped with a foot.
MANAGEMENT. Too descriptive! What about the process!

REVISION 6. Allotment appendages for mice will be: Four leg-foot assemblies, one tail. Deviation from this policy is not permitted as it would constitute inefficient distribution of scarce appendage assets.
MANAGEMENT. Too authoritative! No room for creativity!

REVISION 7. Mice have four feet; each foot is attached to a small leg joined integrally with the overall mouse structural sub-system. Also attached to the mouse sub-system is a thin tail, non-functional and ornamental in nature.
MANAGEMENT. Too verbose/scientific. Answer the question!

REVISION 8. Mice have four feet.
MANAGEMENT. Acceptable.

7 **to be/come equipped with s.th.:** mit etwas ausgestattet sein. | 11 **allotment:** Zuteilung. | 12 **assembly:** hier: Anordnung, Einheit. | **deviation:** Abweichen, Abweichung. | 13 **to constitute:** darstellen, sein. | 14 **scarce:** knapp. | **asset:** hier: Aktivposten, Vermögenswert. | 15 **authoritative:** gebieterisch, bestimmt. | 17 **integrally:** vollständig, ganz. | 20 **verbose:** wortreich, langatmig.

How to Say Nothing at All, yet Sound Competent

Are you the manager of an important company? Are you having trouble convincing your employees that your ideas are good? The COMPETENCE-COMPLEXITY-CONVERTER is just what you need. This useful tool will help you sound like you know what you're talking about. It's easy to use. It works like this:

- Think of any three-digit number.
- Select the corresponding word from each column.

And voilà, you have a term that makes you believable. Take the number 257, for example. Check the COMPETENCE-COMPLEXITY-CONVERTER and you have 'systematized logistical projection'.

We think you will agree that this is a phrase that can be included in virtually any report. It sounds authoritative – and no one will have any idea what you're talking about. More importantly, no one will dare to admit it. The tool can also be used at meetings. If someone asks you a difficult question, simply ask *them* if their question refers to the 'functional logistical time-phrase' (456) or 'optional monitored flexibility' (621).

10 **column:** Spalte. | 16 **virtually:** praktisch, so gut wie. | **to sound authoritative:** Respekt einflößen.

COMPETENCE-COMPLEXITY-CONVERTER

0. integrated	0. management	0. options
1. heuristic	1. organizational	1. flexibility
2. systematized	2. monitored	2. capability
3. parallel	3. reciprocal	3. mobility
4. functional	4. digital	4. programming
5. responsive	5. logistical	5. scenarios
6. optional	6. transitional	6. time-phase
7. synchronized	7. incremental	7. projection
8. compatible	8. 3rd generation	8. hardware
9. futuristic	9. policy	9. contingency

What Academic Writing Really Means ...

Confused by academic writing? This table will help you decipher what those professors and researchers are hiding behind their academic **mumbo-jumbo** (see p. 26).

It has long been known ...	*I couldn't be bothered to look up the original reference.*
A definite trend is evident ...	*These data are practically meaningless.*
Of great theoretical and practical importance ...	*I think this is really interesting.*

13 **table:** hier: Tabelle. | 13 f. **to decipher** [dɪ'saɪfə]: entziffern. |
16 **I couldn't be bothered:** ich hatte keine Lust.

While it has not been possible to provide definite answers to these questions …	*The experiment was a failure, but I still hope to get it published.*
Three of the samples were chosen for detailed study …	*The other results didn't make any sense.*
Typical results are shown …	*This is the nicest graph.*
These results will be shown in a subsequent report …	*I might get around to this sometime.*
It is believed that …	*I think.*
It is generally believed that …	*A couple of other people think so, too.*
It is clear that much additional work will be required before we reach a complete understanding of the phenomenon …	*I don't understand it.*
Correct to within certain tolerance levels …	*Wrong.*
In my experience …	*Once.*
In case after case …	*Twice.*
In a series of cases …	*Three times.*
According to statistical analysis …	*Rumour has it.*

6 **graph:** Schaubild, Diagramm. | 8 **subsequent:** (nach)folgend, später. | 21 **rumour has it:** Gerüchten zufolge.

A statistically oriented projection of the significance of these findings …	*A wild guess.*
Thanks are due to Joe Smith for assistance with the experiment and to George Jones for valuable discussions …	*Smith did the work and Jones explained it to me.*
It is hoped that this study will stimulate further investigation in this field …	*I can't be bothered to do any more work on this topic.*

Academic Article Reconstruction Kit[21]

There are whole books on English for Academic Purposes. But why read them? Just use the Academic Article Reconstruction Kit! For example, using the combination 3462 gives you the following piece of elegant academic prose:

Similarly, our fully integrated field program presents a valuable challenge showing the necessity for improved subcultural compatibility-testing.

Choose a phrase from each group and discover your talent for academic writing!

21 This is a lightly edited version of a document which was circulated in the 1970s.

3 **finding:** Ergebnis. | 12 **kit:** Ausrüstung.

A

0. Obviously,
1. On the other hand,
2. From the intercultural standpoint,
3. Similarly,
4. As Lévi-Strauss contends,
5. In this regard,
6. Based on my own field work in Guatemala,
7. For example,
8. Thus, within given parameters,
9. In respect to essential departmental goals,

B

0. a large proportion of intercultural communicative coordination
1. a constant flow of field-collected input ordinates
2. the characterization of critically co-optive criteria
3. initiation of basic charismatic subculture development
4. our fully integrated field program
5. any exponential anthropological coefficient
6. any further and associated contradictory element
7. the incorporation of agnostic cultural constraints
8. my proposed independent structuralistic concept
9. a primary interrelationship between systems and/or subsystems logistics

6 **to contend:** behaupten. | 7 **in this regard:** in dieser Hinsicht. | 21 **incorporation:** Einbeziehung, Eingliederung. | **constraint:** Zwang.

C

0. must utilize and be functionally interwoven with
1. maximizes the probability of project success while minimizing cross-cultural shock elements in
2. adds explicit performance contours to
3. necessitates that coagulative measures be applied to
4. requires considerable further performance analysis and computer studies to arrive at
5. is holistically compounded, in the context of
6. presents a valuable challenge showing the necessity for
7. recognizes the importance of other disciplines, while taking into account
8. effects a significant implementation of
9. adds overwhelming heuristic significance to

D

0. Propp's basic formulation.
1. the anticipated epistemological repercussions.
2. improved subcultural compatibility testing.
3. all deeper structuralistic conceptualization.
4. any communicatively programmed computer techniques.
5. the profound meaning of *The Raw and the Cooked*.
6. our hedonic regressive perspectives over a given time period.
7. any normative concept of the linguistic/holistic continuum.
8. the total configurational rationale.
9. Krapp's Last Tape.

2 **to interweave with** (fig.): vermischen mit (*interweave – interwove – interwoven*). | 6 **to necessitate:** erforderlich machen, erfordern. | **coagulative:** Gerinnung verursachend. | 11 f. **to take into account:** berücksichtigen, beachten. | 17 **epistemological:** erkenntnistheoretisch. | **repercussion:** Auswirkung. | 25 **rationale:** Grundprinzip.

Virtual Language

The www (world wide wait) has become part of our everyday lives. Some people spend their time egosurfing – scanning the net for their names, while others spend it txtng.

%-(confused
:-o shocked, amazed
:-] sarcastic
:*) drunk
8-) cool, wearing sunglasses
:-@ screaming
;-(crying
;-) winking
:-(sad
:-) happy

Spelling and Texting

When your computer automatically 'miscorrects' your spelling it is referred to as the 'Cupertino Effect'. This term comes from early spellcheckers that automatically 'corrected' the word 'cooperation' into 'Cupertino', the city in California where Apple has its headquarters.

Ode to a Spell Chequer

I have a spelling chequer
It came with my PC
It plainly marks for my revue
miss takes I cannot see
I've run this poem threw it
I'm shore your pleased two no
its letter perfect in its weigh
my chequer tolled me sew.

CU l8r?

Texting is becoming more common than talking on the phone. But for non-texters, it can be like learning another language.

Some common texting abbreviations:

aamof	as a matter of fact
afaik	as far as I know
asap	as soon as possible
b4	before
btw	by the way
cu	see you

ez	easy
f2f	face to face
fyi	for your information
gtg	got to go
jgi	just Google it
imho	in my humble opinion
l8	late
lol	laugh(ing) out loud
nbd	no big deal
np	no problem
nsfw	not safe for work
omg	oh my god
otoh	on the other hand
plz	please
rofl	roll on the floor laughing
sup	what's up
thx	thanks
wtf	what the f---?
yolo	you only live once

A poem submitted to a competition using the latest mobile phone technology:[22]

I no ur gr8
So I cn hardly w8
2 cum 2 yr plc
& c u f2f

22 This poem was entered in the *Guardian's* Text Poetry Competition.

20 **to submit to:** einreichen bei.

Texting advice:
Avoid 'flaming' because USING CAPITAL LETTERS MAKES YOU LOOK ANGRY SO YOU SHOULD NOT DO IT UNLESS YOU REALLY ARE FURIOUS.

The Internet

Choosing a name for your new website can be a challenge. Here are some examples which were not terribly well thought out.

penisland.net
Buy pens and other wares at 'Pen Island'.

therapistfinder.com
Find someone to talk to.

choosespain.com
It can't hurt to check out Spain for your next holiday.

partnerstalking.com.au
Do you feel ignored by your partner? Here's a good place to feel noticed.

whorepresents.com
Need representation? This is the site for you.

expertsexchange.com
Experts come here all the time.

2 **flaming:** Flamen (verbales Attackieren bei der schriftlichen Kommunikation im Internet). | 18 **whorepresents:** **1.** *whore* (Hure) *presents*; **2.** *who represents.*

powergenitalia.com
Pay your electricity bills online. Check PowerGen Italy's website for details.

speedofart.com
Looking for new art in a hurry? Try Speed of Art.

childrenswear.co.uk
For the latest children's trends.

americanscrapmetal.com
Great prices for your waste.

4 **speedofart: 1.** *speedo* (Schwimmanzug) *fart* (Furz); **2.** *speed of art.* | 8 **americanscrapmetal: 1.** *Americans crap* (scheißen) *metal;* **2.** *American scrap metal* (Altmetall).

Games

Game 1

Idioms human body: similar idioms in both languages (see p. 67 f.)

Provide the correct preposition to complete the idiom: *on, behind, out of, off, off, from.*

(1) to laugh your head __________ (sich kaputtlachen)

(2) ________________ the tip of your tongue (liegt mir auf der Zunge)

(3) to have someone eating ____________________ the palm of your hand (jemand frisst dir aus der Hand)

(4) wet ____________________ the ears (feucht hinter den Ohren)

(5) to shoot ____________________ the hip (aus der Hüfte schießen)

(6) to talk someone's ear __________ (jemandem ein Ohr abkauen)

Game 2

Idioms human body: same meaning, different idioms (see p. 68 f.)

Provide the correct body part to complete the idiom: *nose, foot, fingers, thumb, neck, feet, hand, lip.*

(1) to cross your ______________ (die Daumen drücken)

(2) to have two left ________________ (zwei linke Hände haben)

(3) to get your ________________ bent out of shape (eine beleidigte Leberwurst sein)

(4) to stick/put your ________________ in your mouth (ins Fettnäpfchen treten)

(5) to know something/somewhere like the back of your ________________ (etwas wie seine Westentasche kennen)

(6) to keep a stiff upper ________________ (die Ohren steif halten)

(7) to stick your ________________ out for someone (sich für jemanden aus dem Fenster lehnen)

(8) to stick out like a sore ________________ (auffallen wie ein bunter Hund)

Game 3, Part 1

Common sounds in the environment (see p. 30 ff.)

Use these verbs appropriately: *bang, sizzle, tick, jingle, hiss, drip, crash, pop, squeak, buzz.*

(1) She could hear the clock on the wall ________________.

(2) He needed to repair the faucet because they kept hearing the water ________________.

(3) On the 4th of July, the fireworks light up the sky and people can hear them ________________.

(4) He heard the cars ____________ in an accident at the corner.

(5) I knew the water was boiling because I could hear the kettle ____________.

(6) At the celebration you could hear lots of champagne corks ____________.

(7) I knew it would be good breakfast because I could smell the bacon and hear it ____________.

(8) She always knew when her husband walked through the door because she could hear his keys ____________ ____________.

(9) That bicycle is driving me crazy because both wheels ____________.

(10) You know it is summer when you can hear the bees ____________ around their hive.

Game 3, Part 2

Less common sounds in the environment (see p. 30 ff.)
Use these verbs appropriately: *screech, thud, crack, roar, whir, crunch, swish, gurgle, clank, squeak.*

(1) At the private airport, you can hear the airplane propellers ____________.

(2) On their driveway, the car tires ____________ ____________ on the gravel as you pull in.

23 **gravel:** Kies. | **to pull in:** hineinfahren.

(3) She likes their new house, but she hates the way cars go around the corner too fast and the tires ______________.

(4) When she comes home from school and she drops her heavy backpack on the floor, you can hear it ______________.

(5) The waiter poured the water so slowly that you could not hear it ______________.

(6) There were so many flies at the stable that the poor horses constantly ______________ their tails.

(7) Old doors typically ______________ if you don't oil them.

(8) She enjoyed the smell of the ocean and she liked to listen to the waves ______________.

(9) The horse ran away when it heard the whip ______________.

(10) When the old gate blew open, you could hear the metal chain ______________ in the wind.

Game 4

Euphemisms (see p. 105 ff.)

Match the taboo verb with the euphemistic verb.

to die	to get the axe
to masturbate	to have a bun in the oven
to have sex	to be off your rocker

8 **stable:** Stall.

to be pregnant	to toss your cookies
to go to the toilet	to cut the cheese
to fart	to answer the call of nature
to vomit	to spank the monkey
to be crazy	to go all the way
to get fired	to kick the bucket
to have diarrhoea	to have the runs

Game 5

Collective nouns for people (see p. 79 f.)

Match the collective noun to the correct group.

1. a pack of	singers
2. a gang of	angels
3. a den of	athletes
4. a bunch of	pilots
5. a team of	angry protesters
6. a bus-load of	liars
7. a crowd of	beauties
8. a mob of	actors
9. a choir of	thieves
10. a bevy of	tourists
11. a congregation of	street kids
12. a company of	idiots
13. a squadron of	dancers
14. a host of	churchgoers
15. a troupe of	people

Game 6

Collective nouns for animals (see p. 76 f.)

Fill in the correct collective noun: *pack, colony, herd, mob, pride, school, flock, litter, swarm, pod.*

1. Fish swim in a ____________________ .
2. Cattle roam in a ____________________ .
3. Birds fly in a ____________________ .
4. Wolves move in a ____________________ .
5. Lions live in a ____________________ .
6. Ants work in a ____________________ .
7. Whales swim in a ____________________ .
8. Kittens and puppies are born in a __________ .
9. Kangaroos jump in a ____________________ .
10. Bees fly in a ____________________ .

Keys

Game 1

1. to laugh your head **off**
2. **on** the tip of your tongue
3. to have someone eating **out of** the palm of your hand
4. wet **behind** the ears
5. to shoot **from** the hip
6. to talk someone's ear **off**

Game 2

1. to cross your **fingers**
2. to have two left **feet**
3. to get your **nose** bent out of shape
4. to stick/put your **foot** in your mouth
5. to know something/somewhere like the back of your **hand**
6. to keep a stiff upper **lip**
7. to stick your **neck** out for someone
8. to stick out like a sore **thumb**

Game 3, Part 1

1. clocks **tick**
2. water **drips**
3. fireworks **bang**
4. cars **crash**
5. kettles **hiss**
6. champagne corks **pop**
7. bacon **sizzles**
8. keys **jingle**
9. wheels **squeak**
10. bees **buzz**

Game 3, Part 2

1. propellers **whir**
2. car tires on gravel **crunch**
3. tires **screech**
4. heavy objects **thud**
5. water **gurgles**
6. horses' tails **swish**
7. doors **creak**
8. waves **roar**
9. whips **crack**
10. chains **clank**

Game 4

to die	to kick the bucket
to masturbate	to spank the monkey
to have sex	to go all the way
to be pregnant	to have a bun in the oven
to go to the toilet	to answer the call of nature
to fart	to cut the cheese
to vomit	to toss your cookies
to be crazy	to be off your rocker
to get fired	to get the axe
to have diarrhoea	to have the runs

Game 5

1. a pack of	liars
2. a gang of	street kids
3. a den of	thieves
4. a bunch of	idiots
5. a team of	athletes
6. a bus-load of	tourists
7. a crowd of	people
8. a mob of	angry protesters

9. a choir of — singers
10. a bevy of — beauties
11. a congregation of — churchgoers
12. a company of — actors
13. a squadron of — pilots
14 a host of — angels
15. a troupe of — dancers

Game 6

1. a school of — fish
2. a herd of — cattle
3. a flock of — birds
4. a pack of — wolves
5. a pride of — lions
6. a colony of — ants
7. a pod of — whales
8. a litter of — kittens/puppies
9. a mob of — kangaroos
10. a swarm of — bees

We hope you've had as much fun reading this book as we had writing it!

For Further Fun

Berlitz, Charles, *Native Tongues*, New York: Grosset & Dunlap, 1982.
Byrne, Robert, *1,911 Best things anybody ever said*, New York: Fawcett Columbine, 1988.
Davies, John (ed.), *Everyman's Book of Nonsense*, London: Dent, 1981.
Lederer, Richard, *Anguished English*, New York: Dell, 1987.

Editorische Notiz

Der Text verwendet sowohl britisches als auch amerikanisches Englisch. Das Glossar erklärt in der Regel alle Wörter, die im *Thematischen Grund- und Aufbauwortschatz Englisch* von Gernot Häublein und Recs Jenkins (Stuttgart: Ernst Klett Sprachen GmbH, 2009) nicht enthalten sind.

Im Glossar verwendete englische Abkürzungen

AE	American English
arch.	archaic (veraltet)
BE	British English
coll.	colloquial (umgangssprachlich)
fig.	figurative (figurativ, übertragen)
form.	formal
pej.	pejorative (abwertend)
pl.	plural
sl.	slang
s.o.	someone
s.o.'s	someone's
s.th.	something
vulg.	vulgar
zool.	zoological